A Simple Way to Pray

The Wisdom of Martin Luther on Prayer

Archie Parrish

Foreword by R. C. Sproul

A Simple Way to Pray

Published by Serve International, Inc.
P.O. Box 71716
Marietta, GA 30005
www.KingdomPrayer.org

Fifth Edition 2009

The Way to Pray by Martin Luther (chapter 3) was translated from German to English by S. W. Singer, London, 1846, and is reprinted from Luther's *Works, Vol. 43*, edited by Gustav Wiencke, © 1968 Fortress Press. Used by permission of Augsburg Fortress. Some minor edits have been made to conform the text to modern punctuation and spelling conventions.

Printed in the United States of America
ISBN 1-930976-07-0

For more than forty years, I have served the Lord in ministry that has taken me to almost fifty countries on every continent, where I have known many leaders in business, government, and the church. When I considered to whom this presentation on Martin Luther's prayer life should be dedicated, many names came to mind. One stood out above all the rest. I have known and worked with R. C. Sproul for more than thirty years. I have found him to be a brilliant, bold, and passionate champion for biblical truth. He is more like Luther than any other person I have known.

So it is with great admiration and affection that I dedicate *A Simple Way to Pray* to

Dr. R. C. Sproul.

Contents

Foreword

I like to think of Martin Luther as a personal friend. Of course, I never met him since he lived centuries before I was born. And even if I had been alive and living in Germany during his tenure there, it is certain that I would not have been worthy of being considered his personal friend. In the land of Luther, I would have been a Lilliputian in the midst of giants.

Luther has become my friend as a pen pal gets to know another person. By reading his works, his letters, his sermons, and so forth I have, as it were, eavesdropped on the man—if it is possible to eavesdrop by reading.

In his manifold writings, Luther revealed not only his thought but also himself. One thing screams through his pages: he was a man who not only delighted in prayer, but one who clung desperately to this means of grace. Luther lived daily exposed to what he called the *Anfectung*—the unbridled, vicious assault of Satan. At times, it seemed as if the whole world was against him, not to mention the flesh and the Devil.

In his penchant for bombast, Luther occasionally comes across like a child who whistles when he passes a cemetery in the dark. Beneath the Teutonic exterior beat the heart of a man who hung by his fingernails to the hope of the gospel.

A portion of the prayer Luther composed on the eve of his final meeting at the Diet of Worms is contained in this book. In this prayer, we observe Luther naked before God, enduring his private Gethsemane. His prayer reveals the man.

At many points in my own spiritual pilgrimage, the writings of Luther have brought me comfort and encouragement. When I am downcast, I think of Melanchthon's words: "Sing the 46th"—a call to sing Luther's "A Mighty Fortress Is Our God," based on Psalm 46.

Yet, of all the writings of Luther, none has touched me more deeply than his *A Simple Way to Pray*, later renamed *The Way to Pray*. It has been an *open sesame* for me. Of course, Luther was a Lutheran. But in this little book, he becomes for a season a true Methodist. He gives us a practical *method* for effective prayer.

By this method, this enriching approach to prayer, I am helped every day of my life. I love to pray through the Lord's Prayer, the Decalogue, and the Apostles' Creed. I love to use the Psalms to deepen my prayer life.

When we get on our knees, we are all simple men. As simple people, we need a simple way to pray. There is a huge, unbridgeable chasm between the simple and the simplistic. There is nothing simplistic about this spiritual endeavor. Rather it is a simple way to sound the deep things of God.

—*R. C. Sproul*
Orlando, Florida
2002

For a catalog of Christian resources from Dr. Sproul's ministry, contact:

Ligonier Ministries
P.O. Box 863595
Orlando, FL 32886-3595
www.ligonier.org
800-435-4343

Preface to the Fourth Edition

Martin Luther's advice to his barber about prayer has been available in his *Works* for more than four hundred years. Thousands of people have received great benefit by reading it. Serve International developed this little book for use in its process of Kingdom-focused Prayer discipleship. Many of those who have participated in this process have provided feedback. This feedback prompted us to develop this improved and enlarged edition.

There are four significant improvements in this edition:

1. We have put this edition of *A Simple Way to Pray* into the context of Luther's life. Have your ever heard the saying that a text out of its context is a pretext? In Christian circles, this has become a cliché, but it is true. Some previous readers of Luther's little book began to recite the Lord's Prayer, the Ten Commandments, and the Apostle's Creed as a magic formula, but nothing significant happened in their "prayer lives." In this edition we have added a brief discussion of seven disciplines Luther practiced that provide the context for his *A Simple Way to Pray.*

2. We have added a chapter on praying the psalms. In *The Way to Pray*, Luther said he warmed his heart with psalms. Many previous readers asked how he did this.

So we have drawn information from his *Works* and other sources to answer this question. We have also drawn on a twentieth century German disciple of Luther, who provides insight and practical help in praying the Psalms.

3. We have added a chapter dealing with prayer as a spiritual discipline in the context of the additional disciplines of solitude, silence, listening, meditating, journaling, and obeying. Luther's life shows the significant role of these spiritual disciplines.

4. We have developed accompanying free guides for group discussion facilitators and participants. For about two years, we have been developing guides to help in the group discussion of this material. Group discussion enables individual believers to transform the data in this book into life-transforming practice. This tool and the process we recommend for using it are not perfect, nor will they ever be. But the book you are now reading is better than it has been because it has been improved by people like you who have actually used it. Furthermore, this tool and the process we recommend for using it will be further improved as you share your concerns and questions with us by means of our Web page,
www.kingdomprayer.org.

Acknowledgments

How can I thank everyone who has helped me on this book, since the first edition to this fifth edition and printing?

Most significant is Jean, my wife and partner in ministry for more than fifty-five years.
Contributing to this latest edition were Greg Bailey, through his editorial skills, and J.C. Poole, who redesigned the book and oversaw the printing. This book has been significantly improved by past coworkers such as Stewart and Julie Anne Cross and Gary and Diane Hitzfeld. I also am very grateful to Mandy Hammon and Brittany Graffagnino my personal assistants. I appreciate all who have used this material and helped improve it, even though there is not room here to list all their names. I am also grateful to the Cecil Day Foundation and its director, Woody White. I especially want to thank the Serve International Board of Directors: Rencher Gutteridge, William Hollberg, Rich Gartrell, John Wise, Richard Hostetter, and R. C. Sproul. These men hold a special place in my heart. They have prayed for and with me, and together we have won many battles.

I thank all of you and pray that the Lord will richly bless each of you.

Chapter 1

Martin Luther, a Man of Prayer

We can find many examples of men who understood and enjoyed a life rich with prayer, but Martin Luther stands as a giant among them.

In his classic work on prayer, Friedrich Heiler declares, "After Jeremiah, Jesus, and Paul, the German reformer is indeed the most powerful among the eminent men who had a genius for prayer."[1] Indeed, Luther spent much of his time in prayer; the historical records show that he prayed four hours each day. Helmut Thieliche wrote "Luther prayed this much, not despite his busy life, but because only so could he accomplish his gigantic labors. . . . To work without praying and without listening means only to grow and spread oneself upward, without striking roots and without creating an equivalent in the earth. A person who works this way is living unnaturally."[2] From these comments, we can begin to see the kind of prayer that was a vital part of Luther's life.

Before we discuss Luther's prayer life further, let me deal with a question that sometimes comes up: Is Luther a valid model of a praying believer for *all* Christians? Once, when I was leading a Kingdom Intercessors' Training event, a physician said: "I can't identify with Luther—nor do I identify with you. Both you and Luther are clergy. Clergy are not normal people who live in the same world that I live in. How does an *ordinary* person like me in the *real* world become a man of prayer?"

The doctor's question reflects a common tendency to place spiritual leaders in a category by themselves. The Bible does not do this. Consider Elijah: "Elijah was a man with a nature like ours, and he prayed earnestly that it would not rain; and it did not rain on the land for three years and six months. And he prayed again, and the heaven gave rain, and the earth produced its fruit" (James 5:17–18). Or consider the apostles Peter and John: although they were "uneducated and untrained men," they drew attention because of their courage, and it was noted that "they had been with Jesus" (Acts 4:13). To the Corinthians, Paul wrote:

> For you see your calling, brethren, that not many wise according to the flesh, not many mighty, not many noble, are called. But God has chosen the foolish things of the world to

14

put to shame the wise, and God has chosen the weak things of the world to put to shame the things which are mighty; and the base things of the world and the things which are despised God has chosen, and the things which are not, to bring to nothing the things that are, that no flesh should glory in His presence. (1 Cor. 1:26–29)

God usually chooses what is foolish in the world to shame the wise. But Luther is an example of a man, wise according to the world, whom God chose for a specific purpose. Luther occupies a unique place in the history of the German people. Among the British, there is no one person like Luther. No Englishman had anything like Luther's range. In his book, *Here I Stand: A Life of Martin Luther*, Roland H. Bainton writes: "The Bible translation in England was the work of Cranmer, the catechism of the Westminster divines. The sermonic style stemmed from Latimer; the hymnbook came from Watts. And not all of these lived in the same century. Luther did the work of more than five men. And for sheer richness and exuberance of vocabulary and mastery of style he is to be compared only with Shakespeare."[3]

The overwhelming majority of believers are ordinary people similar to the apostles. However, God still calls geniuses, and when He calls He expects them to serve with humility and acknowledge that He is the source of all their ability. If you, like Luther, are among the few wise human beings, I pray that God will keep you humble. Don't depend on yourself. My advice to all who read this book is *use Luther as an example in prayer, but don't try to be Luther.*

The doctor I mentioned above said he couldn't identify with clergy, but Scripture makes it very clear that *God expects the clergy to be examples for all believers* (see 1 Tim. 4:12; Titus 2:6–8). Pastors must be men of high spiritual and moral character (see 1 Tim. 3:1–7; Titus 1:6–9) so that when they multiply after their kind, they will be the kind that should be multiplied. Godly pastors produce godly followers. In this way, God helps parents, politicians, professionals, business leaders, shop workers, secretaries, plumbers, carpenters, and all believers in the marketplace, home, and school to minister as godly men and women in the particular realms where His providence places them.

The bottom line is this: Luther as a man of prayer is a valid example for all Christians.

As you proceed with this study, you will receive insights that will transform your ability to pray. Then you will be more able to commune with the Father, conform to the Son, and combat the forces of evil. In response to your prayers, the Holy Spirit will enable you to minister with greater boldness and power. Using this biblical prayer model will result in increased blessing for you, your family, your church, and the people in your circle of influence.

Luther's Birth and Early Years

Martin Luther was born in Eisleben, in what is now Germany, to good but humble parents. As a child, he dealt with his share of bullies and hard times. Like so many school children in that austere age, he had to earn his livelihood by singing in the streets or by begging from door to door for alms and bread. His father wanted him to become a lawyer, so he was schooled at Mansfeld, Magdeberg, and Eisenach. At age seventeen, he entered the University of Erfurt, where he received his bachelor's degree in 1503 and his master's degree in 1505. Through hard work in school, Luther advanced rapidly.

Then came a turning point in his life. On July 17, 1505, much against his father's wishes, Luther entered the Augustinian monastery at Erfurt. Luther himself preserved complete silence as to his motive, but various legends have arisen to account for this sudden decision. According to one account, on July 2, he was walking with his best friend, Alexis near the village of Stotternheim when a thunderstorm came up and a bolt of lightning struck Alexis dead at his feet. Shocked by his friend's death and suddenly

17

conscience-stricken by the thought of his youthful sins, he was constrained to devote himself to life as a monk.[4]

Prayer in the Time of Martin Luther

The sixteenth-century monastic life in the Church of Rome buried biblical prayer beneath layers of institutional, mystical, and theological error. The Roman Church was centered in the clergy. It taught that the grace of God was dispensed *only* by the Roman Church through priests who were ordained in the succession of Peter. This teaching turned prayer into an institutionalized ritual, making a priest's prayer more valuable than the prayers of laymen. Rome believed that the high and holy God could not be approached directly by average sinners. Rather, the common people must approach God through the priests, who held a privileged position, and the saints, who were exceptionally holy. The Roman Church taught that those who desired to develop lives of holiness should enter monasteries or convents to escape from the wicked world through contemplative prayer. This was the life Luther undertook.

For most monks in the sixteenth century, prayer was a mechanical religious rite, requiring little thought. The faithful confessed their sins and the priest told them what penance they must render, such as how many "Our Fathers" or "Hail Marys" to say. Thus, prayer was a legalistic work that, according to the Roman Church, had merit in itself.

In 1517, Leo X was pope of the Roman Church; Maximilian I, of Austria, governed the Holy Roman Empire; and Frederick, surnamed the Wise, ruled over Saxony. Luther became a monk in the Order of Eremites of St. Augustine. He then became a professor of theology at the University of Wittenberg, which Frederick had established.

Luther was a gifted, hard-working, and eloquent professor. He preferred the truth in the Holy Scriptures and sound reason over any human authorities or opinions. Luther's quest for truth moved to a new level when he nailed his Ninety-five Theses on the church door at Wittenberg. The Ninety-five Theses were theological issues Luther desired to debate, but nailing the Theses to the church door began what eventually grew into a holy war between Luther and the pope. With dauntless courage, he almost entirely alone opposed the power structure of the Roman Church. Many applauded his courage and heroism, but no one, not even Luther, anticipated his success. No one expected that this lightly armed warrior could harm a Hercules whom so many heroes had assailed in vain.

The Confrontation

One of the most significant events in what would become the Protestant struggle took place at Worms, Germany, in 1521. Luther was called to appear before an imperial diet, or court, to answer charges that his teaching was heretical. Luther knew the journey to Worms would be very perilous. His friends urged him not to go, and even the elector, Luther's prince, refused to let him go until he obtained safe passage from the emperor. When he came to the territory of Worms, he would still be in great danger. Luther replied that he would go there even if the devils outnumbered the tiles on the roofs. He was determined to go.

On April 17, 1521, the marshal of the empire escorted Luther, wearing his monk's robes, from his lodgings to the diet. The archbishop of Treves asked him two questions: Would he acknowledge the books that were laid upon a bench before him to be his productions, and would he recant the opinions contained in them? Luther was on the verge of answering "Yes" to the first question when Dr. Jerome Schurf, a jurist of Wittenberg, reminded him that he should first see if there were any books that were not his. After hearing the titles read, he answered that the books were all his. However, at the suggestion of his counselor, he requested that he be allowed until the next day to consider his answer to the second question.

That night in his room, Luther prayed:

> The bell has been already cast, judgment has been pronounced. Ah God, ah God, O You, my God. Stand by me; do this, You must do it, You alone! The matter is not mine, it is Yours. O God, do You not hear? My God, art Thou dead? No, You cannot die; You only hide Yourself. Stand by me. Lord, where do You tarry? Where art You, O my God? Come, come! I am ready, even to forsake my life for this, submissive as a lamb, for righteous is this cause which is Yours. And should my body perish for this cause, should it fall to the ground, yea, be broken to fragments, yet Your Word and Your Spirit are enough. And all this can happen only to the body; the soul is Yours and belongs to You and will remain forever with You.[5]

In the quiet of his room, Luther might have thought about John Hus of Bohemia, who had been burned at the stake for seeking reforms similar to those that he now sought. The words of his prayer show that Luther knew that what he said to the diet the next day might result in a similar sentence for him.

Luther's heart turned to God in Psalm 46, which the psalmist wrote at a time when he saw the world falling apart. At this time of Luther's great crisis, this psalm became a major source of encouragement to him. Psalm 46 reads:

God is our refuge and strength,
A very present help in trouble.
Therefore we will not fear,
Even though the earth be removed,
And though the mountains be carried into the midst
of the sea;
Though its waters roar and be troubled,
Though the mountains shake with its swelling.
Selah.

There is a river whose streams shall make glad the
city of God,
The holy place of the tabernacle of the Most High.
God is in the midst of her, she shall not be moved;
God shall help her, just at the break of dawn.
The nations raged, the kingdoms were moved;
He uttered His voice, the earth melted.

The LORD of hosts is with us;
The God of Jacob is our refuge. Selah.

Come; behold the works of the LORD,
Who has wrought desolations in the earth.
He makes wars cease to the end of the earth;
He breaks the bow and cuts the spear in two;

He burns the chariot in the fire.
Be still, and know that I am God;
I will be exalted among the nations,
I will be exalted in the earth!

The LORD *of hosts is with us;*
The God of Jacob is our refuge. Selah.

At some point, Luther put the truth of this psalm into what became the "Battle hymn of the Reformation":[6]

A mighty fortress is our God,
A bulwark never failing;
Our Helper He amid the flood
Of mortal ills prevailing.
For still our ancient foe
Doth seek to work us woe—
His craft and power are great,
And armed with cruel hate,
On earth is not his equal.

Did we in our own strength confide,
Our striving would be losing,
Were not the right man on our side,
The man of God's own choosing.
Dost ask who that may be?
Christ Jesus, it is He—
Lord Sabaoth His name,

From age to age the same,
And He must win the battle.

And though this world with devils filled,
Should threaten to undo us,
We will not fear, for God has willed
His truth to triumph through us.
The prince of darkness grim,
We tremble not for him—
His rage we can endure,
For lo, his doom is sure:
One little word will fell him.

That word above all earthly powers,
No thanks to them, abideth;
The Spirit and the gifts are ours
Through Him who with us sideth.
Let goods and kindred go,
This mortal life also—
The body they may kill,
God's truth abideth still:
His kingdom is forever.[7]

Fervent prayer through the night was not a new experience for Luther. Before his heart was liberated by the truth of the gospel, he had spent long, solitary night watches in prayer and fasting. These were efforts to gain the favor of God by good works. But when the Spirit set him free, he was free indeed: he became a grace-driven, disciplined soldier of the cross.

On April 18, Luther reappeared before the diet. The question was repeated. Luther answered:

> Some of my writings treat the Christian faith and life, others are directed against the papacy; still others are against private individuals who defend the Romish tyranny and assail holy doctrines. As for the first I cannot renounce them because even my enemies admit that they contain much good matter; nor can I renounce the second because that would help support the papal tyranny. In the third group, I freely admit I have often been too vehement, yet I cannot renounce them unless it can be shown to me that I have gone too far.[8]

The examining official demanded that Luther give a categorical answer. Luther replied, "I cannot [recant] unless I am convinced of error from Scripture and reason."[9]

The official told Luther he must be wrong, because he contradicted the pope and the ecclesiastical councils. Luther answered, "The pope and the ecclesiastical councils have often erred and contradicted themselves." Then he closed with the declaration,

"Here I stand: I can do no more: God help me. Amen."[10]

On May 8, 1521, a bill declaring Luther to be an outlaw was drawn up. This bill declared that after twenty-one days of safe conduct, no man might harbor or conceal Luther on penalty of treason. Luther became a public enemy, wanted throughout Europe dead or alive. Whoever might find him in any place was ordered to apprehend and deliver him to the emperor. All his followers were to be seized wherever they might be found, stripped of all their goods, and imprisoned.

Through his private struggles in prayer at Worms, Luther received from the Lord that unshakable strength, assurance, and confidence that enabled him to defy a world of enemies. God used this man of prayer to begin a great Reformation, a new era in the history of Christianity.[11]

What might it be like to pray with Luther? A study of Luther's prayer reveals a childlike simplicity and love for God blended with streams of joyful trust and surrender to Him. His prayers exude a hot passion that seems to pour from his heart without reserve. He simply, fervently expresses the needs of his heart and conscience. He earnestly cries out to God for comfort, help, and grace.

26

Veit Dietrich, a friend of Luther, describes what it was like to watch him pray:

> What a spirit, what faith, was in his words! He prayed so devoutly, as one who talked with God with the hope and belief of one speaking to his Father. . . . When I heard him at a distance praying in clear tones, my heart burned within me for joy because I heard him speaking in so friendly and reverent a manner with God; chiefly, however, since he leaned so hard upon the promises in the Psalms, as if everything must certainly come to pass which he desired.[12]

The Reformation focused on correcting doctrine and purifying the church, but these achievements could come only after a reformation of prayer. In contrast to the Roman Church of his day, Luther emphasized the priesthood of *all* believers. This biblical prayer empowered the proclamation of the gospel that could purify the church and transform the world.

In the preface to his *Larger Catechism*, Luther writes:

> We know that our defense lies in prayer alone. We are too weak to resist the devil and his vassals. Let us hold fast to the weapons of the

27

Christian; they enable us to combat the devil. For what has carried off these great victories over the undertakings of our enemies which the devil has used to put us in subjection, if not the prayers of certain pious people who rose up as a rampart to protect us?

Our enemies may mock at us. But we shall oppose both men and the devil if we maintain ourselves in prayer and if we persist in it. For we know that when a Christian prays in this way: "Dear Father, Your will be done," God replies to him, "Dear child, yes, it shall be done in spite of the devil and the whole world."[13]

The clarion call of the Protestant Reformation was, "The just shall live by faith" (Rom. 1:17). Faith is, in Luther's judgment, "prayer and nothing but prayer." "He who does not pray or call upon God in his hour of need, assuredly does not think of Him as God, nor does he give Him the honor that is His due."[14]

God, in His sovereign providence, gave Luther extraordinary gifts. And Luther was faithful to use these gifts for the body of Christ. We, as part of the body of Christ, continue to grow in grace from his life work and his disciplined example, which is best seen in his words on prayer.

Chapter 2

Advice for a Barber

One of Martin Luther's oldest and best friends was his barber, Peter Beskendorf, known throughout the town of Wittenberg as Peter, the Master Barber. In a letter to Christopher Scheurl in 1517, Luther included special greetings from Master Peter. So in 1535, the year Luther wrote *The Way to Pray*, Peter had known Luther for eighteen years or more. The barber, who had been a surgeon to Prince Joachim of Anhalt, was known and respected by the Wittenberg University professors.

As Luther's barber, Peter probably enjoyed many conversations with the Reformer. Once, Peter declared that he was going to write a book. He said it would be a book to warn everyone against the power and cunning of the Devil. Luther picked up a book of Peter's and wrote a verse from John 8 about the Devil being a liar and murderer. To this he added forty lines of humorous verse, beginning:

No one will become that sharp
That he can know the devil well.
No, tarred he'll be with his own brush,
And will not in peace be left
Unless Christ is there behind him.[15]

Luther appreciated that Peter was a serious and devout man, so when the barber requested that Luther teach him a simple way to pray that an ordinary man could use, Luther wrote a thirty-four-page book dedicated to "a good friend . . . Peter, the Master Barber." In it, Luther outlined a method for personal devotion that he used himself and recommended as a pattern for developing the discipline of personal devotion.

Luther based his suggestions on the structure and content of his *Small Catechism,* which he wrote in 1529 and regarded as one of his chief accomplishments as an author. *Catechism* has become a specialized word, but it is derived from a word with the simple meaning "to teach by word of mouth" (see the *American Heritage Dictionary* etymology). A catechism, then, is a series of questions and answers intended to teach by word of mouth the foundational truths of the Christian faith. The *Small Catechism* was intended to be simple for use with children. *The Way to Pray* reveals Luther's lifelong use of this writing, not as a textbook for doctrine, but as a daily resource for prayer.

Luther wrote the questions and answers of the *Small Catechism* to teach truths that are central to the faith. His practice of praying these foundational truths enabled him to connect doctrine and devotion like inhaling and exhaling. In his preface to his *Larger Catechism*, which was his expanded set of questions and answers for the more mature, Luther scolded even pastors who might think they were wiser than God in their own eyes because they thought praying the catechism was beneath them. Luther knew from practice that *real faith* was very simple.

Straightforwardly and clearly, Luther described his own method of prayer as *a simple way*. He would begin by taking his Psalter to his room or, if there were church services that day, to the church. He would read psalms to warm his heart toward God. Then he would begin to pray, whispering the memorized words of the catechism's teachings on the Lord's Prayer, the Ten Commandments, and the Apostles' Creed, elaborating on each portion from the fire kindled in his heart.

Luther recommended a set time for personal devotions, early morning or at night, and warned Master Peter against postponing them for some more urgent business. Above all, he said, using an illustration for Peter's benefit, a Christian must keep his mind on his prayer, just as a barber must watch his razor.

Luther remarked: "As a shoemaker makes a shoe, and a tailor makes a coat, so ought a Christian to pray. Prayer is the daily business of a Christian."[16] He saw himself coming to God in prayer as a beggar "who opens wide his cloak in order to receive much." He added, "Prayer is the day's first worship service to God." Luther felt that prayer is "calling on God in heat"[17] because it is living, powerful, strong, mighty, earnest, serious, troubled, passionate, vehement, fervent, and ardent.

Luther would first take each part of the Lord's Prayer with a brief meditation that related to the text of the catechism and to a current situation of his time. For the parts of the catechism that focused on the Ten Commandments, Luther suggested a fourfold way of meditating on each item: first *instruction*, then *thanksgiving*, followed by *confession*, and finally *petition*. He illustrated this process in detail for each commandment. In a later edition, Luther added a section on the Apostles' Creed, extending the fourfold method to that part of the catechism.

Of course, the reader was not meant to repeat Luther's meditative prayers word for word, and Luther stressed that if the Holy Spirit should kindle the heart, all methods and schemes should be abandoned to listen to the "sermon of the Spirit."

Luther was intense, constantly aware of his need for grace, even as he relied on God's grace to discipline his life for prayer. He said prayer is: "The hardest work of all—a labor above all labors, since he who prays must wage almighty warfare against the doubt and murmuring excited by the faintheartedness and unworthiness we feel within us. . . . That unutterable and powerful groaning with which the godly rouse themselves against despair, the struggle in which they call mightily upon their faith."

Luther advised Peter not to attempt to do too much at once:

> Take care not to undertake . . . so much that one becomes weary in spirit. . . . It is enough to consider one section or half a section which kindles a fire in the heart. . . . If in the midst of such thoughts the Holy Spirit begins to preach in your heart with rich, enlightening thoughts, honor Him by letting go of this written scheme; be still and listen to Him who can do better than you can. Remember what He says and note it well and you will behold wondrous things in the law of God.

Luther believed we should come to God in prayer confidently, even boldly. He once said: "If I did not know that our prayer would be heard, the devil may pray in my stead. The Lord is great and high, and therefore He wants great things to be sought from Him and is willing to bestow them so that His almighty power might be shown forth." Because he believed this, Luther prayed: "Dear Lord, I know that You have still more, You have much more than You can ever bestow; in You I shall never want, for if there were need, the heavens would rain guilders [money]. Be my treasury, my cellar, my storehouse; in You have I all riches; if I have You, I have enough."[18]

Luther was specific and active in his requests, saying, "The petitioner should not only present his desire to God," but he should "bolster it well with particulars." As he put it another way, "The petitioner should give motives for his reason; he should seek by every indication and argument to move God to fulfill his wish."

When Luther wrote the book early in 1535, initially titling it *A Simple Way to Pray*. It proved so popular that four editions were printed that year. The last edition, which Luther renamed simply *The Way to Pray*, follows in the next chapter.

As you approach these words, written almost five hundred years ago to a simple Christian just like you, please take a few minutes to pray, asking the Holy Spirit to open your eyes and your heart as He speaks to you through this amazing insight into prayer. It is my prayer for you that you will come to know that when we pray we are not merely saying our prayers, but that we are spending time talking with and listening to our loving Father.

Chapter 3

The Way to Pray,

by

Martinus Luther

For a Good Friend

For Peter, the Master Barber

Dear Master Peter:

I will tell you as best I can what I do personally when I pray. May our dear Lord grant to you and to everybody to do it better than I! Amen.

First, when I feel that I have become cool and joyless in prayer because of other tasks or thoughts (for the flesh and the devil always impede and obstruct prayer), I take my little Psalter, hurry to my room, or, if it be the day and hour for it, to the church where a congregation is assembled and, as time permits, I say quietly to myself and word-for-word the Lord's Prayer, Ten Commandments, the Creed, and, if I have time, some words of Christ or of Paul, or some psalms, just as a child might do.

It is a good thing to let prayer be the first business of the morning and the last at night. Guard yourself carefully against those false, deluding ideas that tell you, Wait a little while. I will pray in an hour; first I must attend to this or that. Such thoughts get you away from prayer into other affairs, which so hold your attention and involve you that nothing comes of prayer for that day.

It may well be that you may have some tasks which are as good or better than prayer, especially in an emergency. There is a saying ascribed to St. Jerome that everything a believer does is prayer, and a proverb says, "Those who work faithfully pray twice." This can be said because believers fear and honor God in their work and remember the commandment not to wrong anyone, or to try to steal, defraud, or cheat. Such thoughts and such faith undoubtedly transform their work into prayer and a sacrifice of praise.

Christ commands continual prayer:

Ask, and it will be given to you; seek, and you

will find; knock, and it will be opened to you. For everyone who asks receives, and he who seeks finds, and to him who knocks it will be opened. If his son asks for bread, will he give him a stone? Or if he asks for a fish, will he give him a serpent? If you then, being evil, know how to give good gifts to your children, how much more will your Father give the Holy Spirit to those who ask Him!" (Luke 11:9–13)

And Paul urges, "Pray without ceasing" (1 Thess. 5:17).

On the other hand, it is also true that the work of unbelievers is outright cursing and so those who work faithlessly curse twice. While they do their work their thoughts are occupied with a neglect of God and violation of His law, how to take advantage of their neighbors, how to steal from them and defraud them. What else can such thoughts be but out-and-out curses against God and humanity, which make such persons' work and effort a double curse by which they curse themselves. In the end, they are beggars and bunglers.

One must unceasingly guard against sin and wrongdoing, something one cannot do unless one fears God and keeps His commandments in mind, as the psalmist says, "Blessed are those . . . who meditate on his law day and night" (Psalm 1:1–2). Yet we must be careful not to break the habit of true prayer and imagine other works to be necessary which, after all, are nothing of the kind. Thus at the end we become lax and lazy, cool and listless toward prayer. The devil who besets us is not lazy or careless, and our flesh is too ready and eager to sin and is disinclined to the spirit of prayer.

When your heart has been warmed by such recitation to yourself (of the Ten Commandments, the words of Christ, etc.) and is intent upon the matter, kneel or stand with your hands folded and your eyes toward heaven and speak or think as briefly as you can:

O heavenly Father, dear God, I am a poor unworthy sinner. I do not deserve to raise my eyes or hands toward You or to pray. But because You have commanded us all to pray and have promised to hear us and through Your dear Son, Jesus Christ, have taught us both how and what to pray, I come to You in obedience to Your Word, trusting in Your gracious promises.

I pray in the name of my Lord Jesus Christ together with all Your saints and Christians on earth as He has taught us:

Our Father in heaven, hallowed be Your name.

40

Your kingdom come. Your will be done on earth as it is in heaven. Give us this day our daily bread. And forgive us our debts, as we forgive our debtors. And do not lead us into temptation, but deliver us from the evil one. For Yours is the kingdom and the power and the glory forever. Amen. (Matthew 6:5-13)

The Lord's Prayer

The First Petition:
"Hallowed be Your name."

Yes, Lord God, dear Father, hallowed be Your name, both in us and throughout the whole world. Destroy and root out the abominations, idolatry, and heresy of all false teachers and fanatics who wrongly use Your name and in scandalous ways take it in vain and horribly blaspheme it. They insistently boast that they teach Your Word and the laws of the church, though they really use the devil's deceit and trickery in Your name to wretchedly seduce many poor souls throughout the world, even killing and shedding much innocent blood, and in such persecution they believe that they render You a divine service.

Dear Lord God, convert and restrain them. Convert those who are still to be converted that they with us and we with them may hallow and praise Your

41

name, both with true and pure doctrine and with a good and holy life. Restrain those who are unwilling to be converted so that they be forced to cease from misusing, defiling, and dishonoring Your holy name and from misleading the poor people. Amen.

The Second Petition:
"Your kingdom come."

O dear Lord, God and Father, You see how worldly wisdom and reason not only profane Your name and ascribe the honor due to You to lies and to the devil, but how they also take the power, might, wealth, and glory which You have given them on earth for ruling the world and thus serving You, and use it in their own ambition to oppose Your kingdom. They are many and mighty; they plague and hinder the tiny flock of Your kingdom who are weak, despised, and few. They will not tolerate Your flock on earth and think that by plaguing them they render a great and godly service to You.

Dear Lord, God and Father, convert them and defend us. Convert those who are still to become children and members of Your kingdom so that they with us and we with them may serve You in Your kingdom in true faith and unfeigned love, and that from Your kingdom which has begun, we may enter into

Your eternal kingdom. Defend us against those who will not turn away their might and power from the destruction of Your kingdom so that when they are cast down from their thrones and humbled, they will have to cease from their efforts. Amen.

The Third Petition:
"Your will be done on earth as in heaven."

O dear Lord, God and Father, You know that the world, if it cannot destroy Your name or root out Your kingdom, is busy day and night with wicked tricks and schemes, strange conspiracies and intrigue, huddling together in secret counsel, giving mutual encouragement and support, raging and threatening and going about with every evil intention to destroy Your name, Word, kingdom, and children. Therefore, dear Lord, God and Father, convert them and defend us. Convert those who have yet to acknowledge Your good will, that they with us and we with them may obey Your will and for Your sake gladly, patiently, and joyously bear every evil, cross, and adversity, and thereby acknowledge, test, and experience Your benign, gracious, and perfect will. But defend us against those who in their rage, fury, hate, threats, and evil desires do not cease to do us harm. Make their wicked schemes, tricks, and devices come to nothing so that these may be turned against them, as we sing, "His mischief returns upon his own head and on his own pate his violence descends."

The Fourth Petition:
"Give us today our daily bread."

Dear Lord, God and Father, grant us Your blessing also in this temporal and physical life. Graciously grant us blessed peace. Protect us against war and disorder. Grant to our dear emperor [a president, prime minister, governor, etc.] fortune and success against his enemies. Grant him wisdom and understanding to rule over his earthly kingdom in peace and prosperity. Grant to all rulers good counsel and the will to preserve their domains and their subjects in tranquility and justice. Amen.

O God, grant that all people—in city and country— be diligent and display charity and loyalty toward each other. Give us favorable weather and good harvest. I commend to You my house and property, wife and children. Grant that I may manage and guide them well, supporting and educating them as a Christian should. Defend us against the Destroyer and all his wicked angels who would do us harm and mischief in this life. Amen.

The Fifth Petition:
"Forgive us our debts, as we forgive our debtors."

O dear Lord, God and Father, enter not into judgment against us because no person living is justified before You. Do not count it against us as a sin that we are so unthankful for Your ineffable goodness, spiritual and physical, or that we stray into sin many times every day, more often than we can know or recognize (see Psalm 19:12). Do not look upon how good or how wicked we have been but only upon the infinite compassion which You have bestowed upon us in Christ, Your dear Son. Amen.

Also, grant forgiveness to those who have harmed or wronged us, as we forgive them from our hearts. They inflict the greatest injury upon themselves by arousing Your anger in their actions toward us. We are not helped by their ruin; we would much rather that they be saved with us. Amen.

The Sixth Petition:
"Lead us not into temptation."

O dear Lord, Father and God, keep us fit and alert, eager and diligent in Your Word and service, so that we do not become complacent, lazy, and slothful as though we had already achieved everything. In that way the fearful devil cannot fall upon us, surprise us, and deprive us of Your precious Word or stir up strife and factions among us and lead us into other sin and disgrace, both spiritually and physically. Rather grant us wisdom and strength through Your Spirit that we may valiantly resist him and gain the victory. Amen.

The Seventh Petition:
"And deliver us from the evil one."

O dear Lord, God and Father, this wretched life is so full of misery and calamity, of danger and uncertainty, so full of malice and faithlessness, as St. Paul says, "The days are evil" (Ephesians 5:16). We might rightfully grow weary of life and long for death. But You, dear Father, know our frailty; therefore help us to pass in safety through so much wickedness and villainy; and, when our last hour comes, in Your mercy grant us a blessed departure from this vale of sorrows so that in the face of death we do not become fearful or despondent but in firm faith commit our souls into Your hands. Amen.

The Amen:

Finally, mark this, that you must always speak the amen firmly. Never doubt that God in His mercy will surely hear you and say yes to your prayers. Never think that you are kneeling or standing alone; rather think that the whole of Christendom, all devout Christians, are standing there beside you and you are

46

standing among them in a common, united petition that God cannot disdain. Do not leave your prayer without having said or thought, Very well, God has heard my prayer; this I know as a certainty and a truth. That is what amen means.

You should also know that I do not want you to recite all these words in your prayer. That would make it nothing but idle chatter and prattle. Rather do I want your heart to be stirred and guided concerning the thoughts that ought to be comprehended in the Lord's Prayer. These thoughts may be expressed, if your heart is rightly warmed and inclined toward prayer, in many different ways and with more words or fewer.

I do not bind myself to such words or syllables, but say my prayers in one fashion today, in another tomorrow, depending upon my mood and feeling. I stay, however, as nearly as I can, with the same general thoughts and ideas. It may happen occasionally that I may get lost among so many ideas in one petition that I forgo the other six.

If such an abundance of good thoughts comes to us we ought to disregard the other petitions, make room for such thoughts, listen in silence, and under no circumstances obstruct them. The Holy Spirit Himself preaches here, and one word of His sermon is far better than a thousand of our prayers. Many times I have learned more from one prayer than I might have learned from much reading and speculation.

It is of great importance that the heart be made ready and eager for prayer. As Sirach says, "Prepare your heart for prayer, and do not tempt God" [Sirach 18:23]. What else is it but tempting God when your mouth babbles and the mind wanders to other thoughts? Like the cleric who prayed, "'Make haste, O God to deliver me' (Psalm 70:1). Farmhand, did you unhitch the horses? 'Make haste, O God, to help me, O Lord' (Psalm 70:1). Maid, go out and milk the cow. Glory be to the Father and to the Son and to the Holy Spirit. Hurry up, boy, I wish the ague would take you!" I have heard many such prayers in the past. This is blasphemy, and it would be better if they played at it if they cannot or do not care to do better. In my day I have prayed many such canonical hours myself, regrettably, and in such a manner that the psalm or the allotted time came to an end before I even realized whether I was at the beginning or the middle.

Though not all of them blurt out the words as did the above-mentioned cleric and mix business and prayer, they do it by the thoughts in their hearts. They jump from one thing to another in their thoughts, and when it is all over they do not know what they have done or what they talked about. They start with Laudate and right away they are in a fool's paradise.

It seems to me that if we could see what arises as prayer from a cold and inattentive heart, we would conclude that we had never seen a more ridiculous kind of buffoonery. But, praise God, it is now clear to me that those who forget what they have said have not prayed well. In a good prayer, one fully remembers every word and thought from the beginning to the end of the prayer.

So a good and attentive barber keeps his thoughts, attention, and eyes on the razor and hair and does not forget how far he has gotten with his shaving or cutting. If he wants to engage in too much conversation or let his mind wander or look somewhere else, he is likely to cut his customer's mouth, nose, or even his throat. Thus if anything is to be done well, it requires the full attention of all one's senses and members, as the proverb says, "The one who thinks of many things, thinks of nothing and does nothing right." How much more does prayer call for concentration and singleness of heart if it is to be a good prayer!

This in short is the way I use the Lord's Prayer when I pray it. To this day I suckle at the Lord's Prayer like a child, and as an old man eat and drink from it and never get my fill. It is the very best prayer, even better than the Psalter, which is so very dear to me.

It is surely evident that a real master composed and taught it. What a great pity that the prayer of such a master is prattled and chattered so irreverently all over the world! How many pray the Lord's Prayer several thousand times in the course of a year, and if they were to keep on doing so for a thousand years they would not have tasted nor prayed one iota, one "jot and tittle" (Matthew 5:18) of it! In a word, the Lord's Prayer is the greatest martyr on earth (as are the name and Word of God). Everybody tortures and abuses it; few take comfort and joy in its proper use.

The Ten Commandments

After praying through the Lord's Prayer, I do the same with the Ten Commandments.[19] I take one part after another and free myself as much as possible from distractions in order to pray.

I divide each commandment into four parts, thereby fashioning a garland of four strands. That is, I think of each commandment as first, instruction, which is really what it is intended to be and consider what the Lord God demands of me so earnestly. Second, I turn it into a thanksgiving; third, a confession; and fourth, a prayer. I do so in thoughts or words such as these:

The First Commandment:
"I am the Lord your God. You shall have no other gods."

Instruction: Here I earnestly consider that God expects and teaches me to trust Him sincerely in all things and that it is His most earnest purpose to be my God. My heart must not build upon anything else or trust in any other thing, be it wealth, prestige, wisdom, might, piety, or anything else.

Thanksgiving: I give thanks for His infinite compassion by which He has come to me in such a fatherly way and, unasked, unbidden, and unmerited, has offered to be my God, to care for me, and to be my comfort, guardian, help, and strength in every time of need. We poor mortals have sought so many gods and would have to seek them still if He did not enable us to hear Him openly tell us in our own language that He intends to be our God. How could we ever—in all eternity—thank Him enough!

Confession: I confess and acknowledge my great sin and ingratitude for having so shamefully despised such sublime teachings and such a precious gift throughout my whole life, and for having fearfully provoked His wrath by countless acts of idolatry. I repent of these and ask for His grace.

Prayer: O my God and Lord, help me by Thy grace to learn and understand Your commandments more fully every day and to live by them in sincere confidence. Preserve my heart so that I shall never again become forgetful and ungrateful, that I may never seek after other gods or other consolation on earth or in any creature, but cling truly and solely to Thee, my only God. Amen, dear Lord God and Father. Amen.

The Second Commandment:
"You shall not make for yourself a carved image."[20]

Instruction: This command teaches that in no way can or may God be visibly portrayed. Although creatures may be portrayed, God forbids making or having such images, if one's intention is to worship them or serve God through them.

We must not try to be wiser than God. He wants His people instructed by the living preaching of His Word—not by idols that cannot even talk. The reasons for this command are that God totally rules over us, that we belong to Him, and He is eager to be worshipped correctly. Therefore, we are to receive and observe and keep pure and entire all such religious worship and ordinances as God has appointed in His Word.

Thanksgiving: I thank God that He has not left me to my own devices for worshipping Him. I thank Him for His gracious direction in Scripture by which I can worship Him in spirit and truth. I thank Him that He is the triune God, above and beyond the imaginations of sinful human beings, and He alone deserves my adoration, praise, and devotion.

Confession: I confess my great sin of idolatry in that I have made a god of my appetites. I am an immoral, impure, greedy, covetous idolater. I brag about shameful things and most of my thoughts are focused on life here on earth. I have not properly esteemed the instruction and living preaching of God's Word. I have not kept pure and entire the worship and ordinances God has appointed in His Word. I repent of these and ask for His mercy and grace.

Prayer: O my God and Lord, help me by Your grace to learn and understand this commandment more fully every day and to live by it in sincere confidence. Deliver me from trying to be wiser than God. Keep me from fearing, loving, or trusting any person or thing as I should fear, love, and trust You. Enable me to delight in the instruction and preaching of Your Word. Help me trust in the Lord with all my heart and lean not on my own understanding. Help me delight that I belong to You and that You totally rule over all Your creation and creatures. Help me receive and observe the worship and ordinances You have appointed in Your Word. Amen.

The Third Commandment:
"You shall not take the name of the Lord your God in vain."

Instruction: I learn that I must keep God's name in honor, holiness, and beauty; not to swear, curse, not to be boastful or seek honor and repute for myself, but humbly to invoke His name, to pray, praise, and extol it, and to let it be my only honor and glory that

He is my God and that I am His lowly creature and unworthy servant.

Thanksgiving: I give thanks to Him for these precious gifts, that He has revealed His name to me and bestowed it upon me, that I can glory in His name and be called God's servant and creature, that His name, as Solomon says, is my refuge like a mighty fortress to which the righteous person can flee and find protection (see Proverbs 18:10).

Confession: I confess and acknowledge that I have grievously and shamefully sinned against this commandment all my life. I have not only failed to invoke, extol, and honor His holy name, but have also been ungrateful for such gifts and have, by swearing, lying, and betraying, misused them in the pursuit of shame and sin. This I bitterly regret and ask grace and forgiveness.

Prayer: I ask for help and strength henceforth to learn to obey this commandment and to be preserved from such evil, ingratitude, abuse, and sin against His name.

The Fourth Commandment:
"Remember the Sabbath day, to keep it holy."

Instruction: I learned from this, first of all, that the

Sabbath day has not been instituted for the sake of being idle or indulging in worldly pleasures, but in order that we may keep it holy. However, it is not sanctified by our works and actions—our works are not holy—but by the Word of God, which alone is wholly pure and sacred and which sanctifies everything that comes in contact with it, be it time, place, person, labor, rest, etc. According to St. Paul, who said that every creature is consecrated by Word and prayer (see 1 Timothy 4:5), our works are consecrated through the Word. I realized, therefore, that on the Sabbath I must, above all, hear and contemplate God's Word. Thereafter, I should give thanks in my own words, praise God for all His benefits, and pray for myself and for the whole world.

Thanksgiving: I thank God in this commandment for His great and beautiful goodness and grace, which He has given us in the preaching of His Word. And He has instructed us to make use of it, especially on the Sabbath day, for the meditation of the human heart can never exhaust such a treasure. His Word is the only light in the darkness of this life, a word of life, consolation, and supreme blessedness. Where this precious and saving word is absent, nothing remains but a fearsome and terrifying darkness, error and faction, death and every calamity, and the tyranny of the devil himself, as we can see with our own eyes every day.

56

Confession: I confess and acknowledge great sin and wicked ingratitude on my part because all my life I have made disgraceful use of the Sabbath and have thereby despised His precious and dear Word in a wretched way. I have been too lazy, listless, and uninterested to listen to it, let alone to have desired it sincerely or to have been grateful for it. I have let my dear God proclaim His Word to me in vain, have dismissed the noble treasure, and have trampled it underfoot. He has tolerated this in His great and divine mercy and has not ceased in His fatherly, divine love and faithfulness to keep on preaching to me and calling me to the salvation of my soul. For this I repent and ask for grace and forgiveness.

Prayer: I pray for myself and for the whole world that the gracious Father may preserve us in His Holy Word and not withdraw it from us because of our sin, ingratitude, and laziness. May He preserve us from divisive spirits and false teachers, and may He send faithful and honest laborers into His harvest (see Matthew 9:38), that is, devout pastors and preachers. May He grant us grace humbly to hear, accept, and honor their words as His own words and to offer our sincere thanks and praise.

The Fifth Commandment:
"Honor your father and your mother."

Instruction: I learn to acknowledge God, my Creator; how wondrously He has created me, body and soul; and how He has given me life through my parents and has instilled in them the desire to care for me, the fruit of their bodies, with all their power. He has brought me into this world, has sustained and cared for me, nurtured and educated me with great diligence, carefulness, and concern, through danger, trouble, and hard work. To this moment He protects me, His creature, and helps me in countless dangers and troubles. It is as though He were creating me anew every moment. But the devil does not willingly concede us one single moment of life.

Thanksgiving: I thank the rich and gracious Creator on behalf of myself and all the world that He has established and assured in the commandment the increase and preservation of the human race, that is, of households and of states. Without these two institutions, or governments, the world could not exist a single year because without government there can be no peace; where there is no peace there can be no family; without family, children cannot be begotten and raised, and fatherhood and motherhood would cease to be.

It is the purpose of this commandment to guard and preserve both family and state, to admonish children and subjects to be obedient and to enforce it too, and to let no violation go unpunished—otherwise children would have disrupted the family long ago by their disobedience, and subjects would have disorganized the state and laid it to waste, for they outnumber parents and rulers. There are no words to fully describe the benefit of this commandment.

Confession: I confess and lament my wicked disobedience and sin; in defiance of God's commandment I have not honored or obeyed my parents; I have often provoked and offended them, have been impatient with their parental discipline, have been resentful and scornful of their loving admonition and have rather gone along with loose company and evil companions. God Himself condemns such disobedient children and withholds from them a long life; many of them succumb and perish in disgrace before they reach adulthood. Whoever does not obey father and mother must obey the executioner or otherwise come, through God's wrath, to an evil end. Of all this I repent and ask for grace and forgiveness.

Prayer: I pray for myself and for all the world, that God would bestow His grace and pour His blessing richly upon the family and the state. Grant that

from this time on we may be devout, honor our
parents, obey our superiors, and resist the devil when
he entices us to be disobedient and rebellious, and so
may we help improve home and nation by our actions
and thus preserve the peace, all to the praise and glory
of God for our own benefit and for the prosperity of
all. Grant that we may acknowledge these His gifts
and be thankful for them.

At this point, we should add a prayer for our
parents and superiors, that God may grant them
understanding and wisdom to govern and rule us
in peace and happiness. May He preserve them from
tyranny, from riot and fury, and turn them to honor
God's Word and not oppress it, nor persecute anyone
or do injustice. Such excellent gifts must be sought
by prayer, as St. Paul teaches; otherwise the devil will
reign in the palace and everything fall into chaos
and confusion.

If you are a father or mother, you should at this point
remember your children and the workers in your
household. Pray earnestly to the dear Father, who
has set you in an office of honor in His name and
intends that you be honored by the name "father."
Ask that He grant you grace and blessing to look
after and support your wife, children, and servants
in a godly and Christian manner. May He give you
wisdom and strength to guide and train them well

in heart and will to follow your instruction with obedience. Both are God's gifts, your children and the way they flourish, that they turn out well and that they remain so. Otherwise the home is nothing but a pigsty and school for rascals, as one can see among the uncouth and godless.

The Sixth Commandment:
"You shall not kill."

Instruction: Here I learn, first of all, that God desires me to love my neighbors, so that I do them no bodily harm, either by word or action, neither injure nor take revenge upon them in anger, vexation, envy, hatred, or for any evil reason, but realize that I am obliged to assist and counsel them in every bodily need. In this commandment God commands me to protect my neighbor's body and in turn commands my neighbor to protect my own.

Thanksgiving: I give thanks for such ineffable love, providence, and faithfulness toward me by which He has placed this mighty shield and wall to protect my physical safety. All are obliged to care for me and protect me, and I, in turn, must behave likewise toward others. He upholds this command and, where it is not observed, He has established the sword as punishment for those who do not live up to it. Were it not for this excellent commandment and ordinance, the devil would instigate such a massacre among us that no one could live in safety for a single hour—as happens when God becomes angry and indicts punishment upon a disobedient and ungrateful world.

Confession: I confess and lament my own wickedness and that of the world, not only that we are so terribly ungrateful for such fatherly love and solicitude toward us—but what is especially scandalous, that we do not acknowledge this commandment and teaching, are unwilling to learn it, and neglect it as though it did not concern us or we had no part in it. We amble along complacently, feeling no remorse that, in defiance of this commandment, we neglect our neighbors, and, yes, we desert them, persecute, injure, or even kill them in our thoughts. We indulge in anger, rage, and villainy as though we were doing a fine and noble thing. Really, it is high time that we started to deplore and bewail how much we have acted like rogues and like unseeing, unruly, and unfeeling persons who kick, scratch, tear, and devour one another like furious beasts and pay no heed to this serious and divine command.

Prayer: I pray the dear Father to lead us to an understanding of this, His sacred commandment, and to help us keep it and live in accordance with it. May He preserve us from the murderer who is the master of every form of murder and violence. May He grant us His grace that we and all others may treat each other in kindly, gentle, charitable ways, forgiving one another from the heart, bearing each other's faults and shortcomings, and thus living together in true peace and concord, as the commandment teaches and requires us to do.

The Seventh Commandment: "You shall not commit adultery."

Instruction: Here I learn once more what God intends and expects me to do, namely, to live chastely, decently, and temperately, both in thoughts and in words and actions, and not to disgrace anyone's spouse, son or daughter, or member of the household. More than this, I ought to assist, save, protect, and guard marriage and decency to the best of my ability. I should silence the idle thoughts of those who want to destroy and slander their reputation. All this I am obliged to do, and God expects me not only to leave the families of my neighbors unmolested, but I owe it to my neighbors to preserve and protect their good character and honor, just as I would want my neighbors to do for me and mine in keeping with this commandment.

Thanksgiving: I thank my faithful and dear Father for His grace and benevolence by which He accepts my wife, son, daughter, and servant into His care and protection, and forbids so sternly and firmly anything that would bring them into disrepute. He protects and upholds this commandment and does not leave violations unpunished, even though He Himself has to act if someone disregards and violates the commandment and precept.

God desires chastity and will not tolerate adultery. That can be seen every day when the impenitent and profligate are overtaken by the wrath of God and perish miserably. Otherwise, it would be impossible to guard one's spouse, children, and servants against the devil's filthiness for a single hour or preserve them in honor and decency. What would happen would be unbridled immorality and beastliness, as happens when God in His wrath withdraws His hand and permits everything to go to wrack and ruin.

Confession: I confess and acknowledge my sin, my own and that of all the world, how I have sinned against this commandment my whole life in thought, word, and action. Not only have I been ungrateful for these excellent teachings and gifts, but I have complained and rebelled against the divine requirement of such decency and chastity, that God has not permitted all sorts of fornication and rascality to go unchecked and unpunished. He will not allow marriage to be despised, ridiculed, or condemned, etc. Sins against this commandment are, above all others, the grossest and most conspicuous and cannot be covered up or whitewashed. For this, I am sorry.

Prayer: I pray for myself and all the world, that God may grant us grace to keep this commandment gladly and cheerfully in order that we might ourselves live in chastity and also help and support others to do likewise.

The Eighth Commandment:
"You shall not steal."

Instruction: First, I can learn here that I must not take property belonging to my neighbors from them or possess it against their will, either in secret or openly. I must not be false or dishonest in business, service, or work, nor profit by fraud, but must support myself by the sweat of my brow and eat my bread in honor. Furthermore, I must see to it that in any of the above-named ways my neighbors are not defrauded just as I wish for myself. I also learn in this commandment that God in His fatherly solicitude sets a protective hedge around my goods and solemnly prohibits anyone to steal from me. Where that is ignored, He has imposed a penalty, and those in authority are ordered to punish the disobedient. Where that cannot be done, God Himself metes out punishment and they become beggars in the end. As the proverb says, "Those who steal in their youth go begging in old age," or "Stolen gain goes down the drain."

Thanksgiving: I give thanks for His steadfast goodness in that He has given such excellent teachings, assurance, and protection to me and to all the world. If it were not for His protection, not a penny or a crumb of bread would be left in the house.

Confession: I confess my sins and ingratitude in such instances where I have wronged, deprived, or cheated anyone in my life.

Prayer: I ask that He grant to me and all the world grace to learn from this commandment, to ponder it, and to become better people, so that there may be less theft, robbery, usury, cheating, and injustice, and that the Judgment Day, for which all saints and the whole creation pray (see Romans 8:20–23), shall soon bring this to an end. Amen.

The Ninth Commandment:
"You shall not bear false witness against your neighbor."

Instruction: This teaches us, first of all, to be truthful to each other, to shun lies and calumnies, to be glad to speak well of each other, and to delight in hearing what is good about others. Thus a wall has been built around our good reputation and integrity to protect it against malicious gossip and deceitful tongues; God will not let those go unpunished, as He has said

66

in the other commandments.

Thanksgiving: We owe Him thanks both for the teachings and the protection that He has graciously provided for us.

Confession: We confess and ask forgiveness that we have spent our lives in ingratitude and sin and have maligned our neighbor with false and wicked talk, though we owe him the same preservation of honor and integrity which we desire for ourselves.

Prayer: We ask for help from now on to keep the commandment, and for a healing tongue.

The Tenth Commandment:
"You shall not covet your neighbor's house.
You shall not covet your neighbor's wife,
or his manservant, or his maidservant, or his cattle,
or anything that is your neighbor's."

Instruction: This teaches us first that we shall not dispossess our neighbors of their goods under pretense of legal claims, or lure away, alienate, or extort what is theirs, but help them to keep what is theirs, just as we wish to be done for ourselves. It is also a protection against the subtleties and chicaneries of shrewd manipulators who will receive their punishment in the end.

Thanksgiving: We should render thanks to Him.

Confession: We should repentantly and sorrowfully confess our sins.

Prayer: We should ask for help and strength devoutly to keep such divine commandments.

These are the Ten Commandments in their fourfold aspect, namely, as a school text, songbook, penitential book, and prayer book. They are intended to help the heart come to itself and grow zealous in prayer. Take care, however, not to undertake all of this or so much that one becomes weary in spirit. Likewise, a good prayer should not be lengthy or drawn out, but frequent and ardent. It is enough to consider one section or half a section, which kindles a fire in the heart. This the Spirit will grant us and continually instruct us in when, by God's Word, our hearts have been cleared and freed of outside thoughts and concerns.

I repeat here what I previously said in reference to the Lord's Prayer: if in the midst of such thoughts the Holy Spirit begins to preach in your heart with rich, enlightening thoughts, honor Him by letting go of this written scheme; be still and listen to Him who can do better than you can. Remember what He says and note it well, and you will behold wondrous things in the law of God (see Psalm 119:18).

Nothing can be said here about the part of faith and Holy Scriptures in prayer because there would be no end to what could be said. With practice, one can take the Ten Commandments on one day, a psalm or chapter of Holy Scripture the next day, and use them as flint and steel to kindle a flame in the heart.

The Apostles' Creed

If you have more time, or the inclination, you may treat the Apostles' Creed in the same manner and make it into a garland of four strands. The creed, however, consists of three main parts or articles, corresponding to the three Persons of the divine majesty, as it has been so divided in the catechism and elsewhere.

The First Article: Creation of the Father
I believe in God, the Father Almighty,
creator of heaven and earth.

Instruction: Here, first of all, a great light shines into your heart if you permit it to and teaches you in a few words what all the languages of the world and a multitude of books cannot describe or fathom in words, namely, who you are, whence you came, and whence came heaven and earth. You are God's creation, His handiwork. That is, of yourself and in yourself you are nothing, can do nothing, know nothing, and are capable of nothing. What were you a thousand years ago? What were heaven and earth before creation? Nothing, just as that which will never be created is nothing. But what you are, know, can do, and can achieve is God's creation, as you confess in the creed by word of mouth. Therefore, you have nothing to boast of before God except that you are nothing and He is your Creator, who can annihilate you at any moment.

Reason knows nothing of such a light. Many great thinkers have sought to know what heaven and earth, people, and animals are, and have found no answer. But here it is declared and faith affirms that God has created everything out of nothing. Here is the soul's garden of pleasure, along whose paths we enjoy the works of God—it would take too long to describe all that.

Thanksgiving: Furthermore, we should give thanks to God that in His kindness He has created us out of nothing and provides for our daily needs out of nothing—has made us to be such excellent beings with body and soul, intelligence, and five senses, and has ordained us to be masters of earth, of fish, bird, and beast, etc. (Here consider Genesis, chapters 1 to 3.)

Confession: We should confess and lament our lack of faith and gratitude in failing to take this to heart, or to believe, ponder, and acknowledge it, and having been more stupid than unthinking beasts.

Prayer: We pray for a true and confident faith that sincerely esteems and trusts God to be our Creator, as this article declares.

The Second Article: Redemption of the Son
And in Jesus Christ, His only Son, our Lord.
He was conceived by the power of the Holy Spirit
and born of the virgin Mary.
He suffered under Pontius Pilate,
was crucified, died, and was buried.
He descended into hell.
On the third day He rose again.
He ascended into heaven,
and is seated at the right hand of the Father.
He will come again to judge the living and the dead.

Instruction: Again, a great light shines forth and teaches us how Christ, God's Son, has redeemed us from death, which, after the creation, had become our lot through Adam's fall and in which we would have perished eternally. Now think: Just as in the first article you were to consider yourself one of God's creatures and not doubt it, now you must think of yourself as one of the redeemed and never doubt that. Emphasize one word above all others, for instance, Jesus Christ, our Lord. Likewise, suffered for us, died for us, arose for us. All this is ours and pertains to us; that us includes yourself, as the Word of God declares.

Thanksgiving: You must be sincerely grateful for such grace and rejoice in your salvation.

Confession: You must sorrowfully lament and confess your wicked unbelief and mistrust of such a gift. Oh, what thoughts will come to mind: the idolatry you have practiced repeatedly, how much you have made of praying to the saints and of innumerable good works of yours which have opposed such salvation.

Prayer: Pray now that God will preserve you from this time forward to the end in true and pure faith in Christ our Lord.

The Third Article: Sanctification of the Spirit
I believe in the Holy Spirit,
the holy catholic Church,
the communion of saints,
the forgiveness of sins,
the resurrection of the body,
and the life everlasting.
Amen.

Instruction: This is the third great light, which teaches us where such a Creator and Redeemer may be found and plainly encountered in this world, and what this will all come to in the end. Much could be said about this, but here is a summary: Where the holy Christian Church exists, there we can find God the Creator, God the Redeemer, God the Holy Spirit, that is, Him who daily sanctifies us through the forgiveness of sins. The Church exists where the Word of God concerning such faith is rightly preached and confessed.

Thanksgiving: Again, you have occasion here to ponder long about everything that the Holy Spirit accomplishes in the Church every day. Therefore, be thankful that you have been called and have come into such a Church.

Confession and Prayer: Confess and lament your lack of faith and gratitude, that you have neglected all this, and pray for a true and steadfast faith that will remain and endure until you come to that place where all endures forever, that is, beyond the resurrection from the dead, in life eternal. Amen.

Chapter 4

Praying the Psalms

It is clear that Martin Luther considered the Lord's Prayer to be one of the most important biblical sources for guidance on prayer. He taught, "A Christian has prayed abundantly who has rightly prayed the Lord's Prayer." Luther further explained: "The Lord's Prayer, the model prayer of Christianity, is exclusively petition. Its contrast with the mystic's prayer is evident, for in the latter, the request is secondary; and if the prayer appears as a petition, this is for the most part a method of expressing mystical communication. The Lord's Prayer is not essentially the prayer of the individual, but a common prayer. It binds people together with one another, so that each prays for the other and with the other."

Luther went so far as to say, "Other prayers should be suspected which do not have or comprise the content and meaning of this prayer."[21]

However, in addition to the Lord's Prayer, Luther taught that the book of Psalms provides invaluable guidance for prayer. Luther found the psalms inexpressibly precious, providing comfort and strength in the trials and conflicts of his life, and he taught that the psalms arm and strengthen believers in their battle against sin and the devil.[22]
He wrote:

> You may rightly call the Psalter a Bible in Miniature, in which all things which are set forth more at length in the rest of the Scriptures are collected into a beautiful manual of wonderful and attractive brevity. From the Psalms you may learn not the works of the saints only, but the words, the utterances, the groans, the colloquies, which they used in the presence of God, in temptation and in consolation; so that though they are dead, in the Psalms they live and speak. The Psalms exhibit the mind of the saints; they express the hidden treasure of their hearts, the working of their thoughts, and their most secret feelings.[23]

Luther especially urged praying of the psalms, saying: "Whoever begins to pray the Psalter earnestly and regularly will *soon take leave* of those other light and personal *little devotional prayers* and say: Ah, there is not the juice, the strength, the passion, the fire which

I find in the Psalter. Anything else tastes too cold and too hard."[24]

Luther's passion for praying the Psalter is evident. As he said in *The Way to Pray*:

> When I feel that I have become cool and joyless in prayer because of other tasks or thoughts (for the flesh and the devil always impede and obstruct prayer), I take my little Psalter, hurry to my room, or, if it be the day and hour for it, to the church where a congregation is assembled and, as time permits, I say quietly to myself and word-for-word the Ten Commandments, the Creed, and, if I have time, some words of Christ or of Paul, or some psalms, just as a child might do.

On the relationship of the Lord's Prayer and the Psalter, Luther said: "It [the Psalter] runs through the Lord's Prayer and the Lord's Prayer runs through it so that it is possible to understand one on the basis of the other and to bring them into joyful harmony."[25]

The Psalms—the Language of Prayer

God blessed my wife and me with three children. From the moment of their births, we talked to them. Daily we did everything we could to get them to repeat what we said. At first, only Jean and I could understand the sounds they made. Day after day, we continued talking to them, and after a while they began echoing our words back to us. Single words grew into short sentences. Because we continued to talk to our children, they learned to talk to us.

In a similar fashion, God teaches His children the language of prayer. The Holy Spirit inspired the whole Bible, and He uses *all* of Scripture, and especially the book of Psalms, to help us pray. Many of the psalms are David's prayers to God, given to us to enlighten and deepen our prayers. Sometimes we feel that we can pray a psalm that seems to fit our situation, but usually we ask the Holy Spirit to enlighten us with the truth of His psalms.

As we pray the psalms, the Holy Spirit enables us to commune with the Father, conform to the Son, and combat the Devil. These three aspects of prayer must be kept in balance. When we commune with the Father, we strengthen our connection with Him as the Holy Spirit uses the Word to show us the Father's power, love, and justice. When we see ourselves as God sees us, the Holy Spirit moves us to conform to the Son. We ask the familiar question, "What would Jesus do?" and we follow His example. This is the vital action for becoming like Him. The more we commune with the Father, the more we want to be conformed to the Son. The more we are conformed to the Son, the more effective we are in spiritual combat. The more we are like Him, the more we oppose evil.

As believers, we are God's adopted children. We are part of His family, the universal church, which gathers all over the world in small groups of local believers. As His sons and daughters, we should live in a conscious, vital relationship with our Father and His family, the local church. Only then can we serve effectively as soldiers in Lord Sabaoth's victorious army and win our battles with the world, the flesh, and the Devil. Then we can sing with Luther, "He must win the battle."[26]

As spiritual warriors, we believe God is sufficient to defeat our enemies; therefore, we boldly engage. This spiritual combat is a test of the spirit and the will, both intense and draining. As we read the psalms, we see how David often struggled with feelings of despair and weakness, and how he turned to God in prayer for strength. Those who would be followers of Jesus need His strength to maintain high morale. This is illustrated by the Calvinist soldiers during the Reformation. W. Stanford Reid explained:

> The leadership and finance could not have won the day had the individual Calvinists not possessed, to quote Cromwell, "a conscience

of what they were doing." In many cases, they won their battles or retrieved those they had lost, not through generalship nor through greater economic power, but because of superior morale. In building up and maintaining this morale, the battle hymns of the Psalter played a conspicuous part.[27]

The Secret of the Psalms

Dietrich Bonhoeffer faced a different kind of battle. A Lutheran pastor in Germany, Bonhoeffer was hanged for helping Jews and opposing Adolf Hitler during World War II. His writings show a singular devotion to living for Christ, and he guides us to a deeper understanding of the psalms as a guide to prayer:

> A psalm that we cannot utter as a prayer, that makes us falter and horrifies us, is a hint to us that here someone else is praying, not we; that the One who is here protesting his innocence, who is invoking God's judgment, who has come to such infinite depths of suffering, is none other than Jesus Christ Himself. He it is who is praying here, and not only here but in the whole Psalter.[28]

Jesus Christ, who was fully God and fully man, can best express the understanding and emotion bound

80

up in the heart of the book of Psalms, Bonhoeffer wrote. Indeed, His story is often told there. Bonhoeffer added:

> This insight the New Testament and the Church have always recognized and declared. The *Man* Jesus Christ, to whom no affliction, no ill, no suffering is alien and who yet was the wholly innocent and righteous one, is praying in the Psalter through the mouth of His Church. The Psalter is the prayer book of Jesus Christ in the truest sense of the word. The Psalter is the vicarious prayer of Christ for His Church. This prayer belongs not to the individual member, but to the whole Body of Christ. In the Psalter we learn to pray on the basis of Christ's prayer.[29]

The Example of Jesus

It was not unusual for devout Jews in the time of Jesus and His apostles to know by heart *the whole of David*, i.e., the entire book of Psalms. It is probable that our Lord Jesus had all the psalms memorized. They certainly were part of the fabric of His life.

In His most painful moments, as He faced death on the cross, He instinctively cried out, "My God, My God, why have you forsaken me?" (Mark 15:34; Matt.

27:46). These were David's very words, as recorded in Psalm 22:1.

Jesus' last words from the cross were, "Father, into Your hands I commit my spirit" (Luke 23:46). As soon as their children began to talk, devout Jewish mothers taught them to pray, "Into Your hand I commit my spirit" (Ps. 31:5). Each night before going to sleep, the children prayed these words. To this childhood prayer, Jesus added the personal address, "Father." Concerning His atoning work on the cross, Jesus declared, "It is finished" (John 19:30); He prayed to the Father as a child lying down to sleep for the night.

The Example of the Early Believers

Paul urged early Christians to "let the word of Christ dwell in you richly, teaching and admonishing one another in all wisdom, singing psalms and hymns and spiritual songs, with thankfulness in your hearts to God" (Col. 3:16). The Christians in the early church took this admonition to heart. Like many devout Jews and the Lord Jesus, many of those believers knew all 150 psalms by heart. In one branch of the Eastern Orthodox Church, this is still a prerequisite for anyone desiring to serve in an ecclesiastical office, such as the pastorate. An early church father, Jerome, said that in his time one could hear psalms being sung in the fields and the gardens. The melody of the

Psalter filled the lives of the early Christians.

David said, "I give myself to prayer" (Psalm 109:4). The original Hebrew literally reads, "I prayer," i.e., "I am prayer." This shows us that the Holy Spirit desires to help us *become* prayer personified, and the psalms can help us in that.

Praying the psalms strengthened the early Christians. New Testament writers quote more verses from the book of Psalms than any other Old Testament book. Praying the Psalter shaped the life of early Christians until they became a force so formidable that they could live, stand, and even die for His coming kingdom.

How to Pray the Psalms

One way to pray the psalms is to read the words aloud in a normal voice or at least in a whisper one verse at a time. This will help you concentrate and avoid distraction., When possible read on your knees. Like young Samuel pray, "Speak, for your servant is listening" (See 1 Sam. 3:9–10, NIV). Pay attention to the prompting of the Spirit to your heart. Discerning the Spirit's prompting in prayer is similar recognizing the voice of your earthly father. You can see an example of this in the preceding chapters of Luther's prayer using the Lord's Prayer. Carry the Psalter with you and refer to it frequently during the day.

Just as you recognize the voice of your earthly father,

you can recognize the Spirit's voice as He leads you in prayer. Listen and obey! You can see an example of this in the preceding chapters of Luther's prayer using the Lord's Prayer.

As you pray, ask the Holy Spirit to show you how to pray for the people on your prayer list: yourself, your family, your friends, your pastor and the leaders of your church, and those around you whose lives you touch who may not have any other contact with the Good News.

In these prayers, you may sometimes *thank* God for the truth expressed in the verse; at other times, you may make a *petition* or request, asking Him to enable you to do what the Holy Spirit tells you to do through the verse. You may *intercede*, asking the Lord to do in another's life what the verse brings to your heart and mind. All these patterns for prayer come to life in the psalms.

One question that often is asked concerning praying psalms is: *How can I pray a psalm when it does not really express what I'm feeling in my heart?* Honest feelings are just that—feelings. We naturally have feelings about our situation, and these feelings are best when they turn us to God for His perspective. As we understand His perspective and His promises, we can honestly admit the need to pray sometimes

84

against our own hearts, in spite of our feelings, in order to pray rightly. We need to pray not what we feel like praying, but what God wants us to pray. Jeremiah warned, "The heart is deceitful above all things, and desperately sick; who can know it?" (Jer. 17:9). If we follow our hearts, we will naturally pray only for our own needs and comforts. "Not the poverty of our heart, but the richness of God's word, ought to determine our prayer."[30] God wants us to pray as Jesus did, that His will be done, not our will. As you pray the psalms, begin by praying, "Father, strengthen my heart and show me how to pray from the richness of Your Word."

The time you take to experience the psalms will enrich your soul and strengthen your faith. As you read through the book of Psalms, keep track of how many psalms you know by heart. You may be surprised how many familiar verses and poems originate in the Psalter. How many would you like to memorize this year? What weekly schedule can you establish to reach this goal? Ask the Father to enable you to learn the psalms by heart. The repetition of memorizing them gives the Holy Spirit a unique opportunity to teach your heart to pray. Use the psalms daily to help yourself grow.

With Luther may we pray: "Our dear Lord, who has given to us and taught us to pray the Psalter and the

Lord's Prayer, grant to us also the spirit of prayer and of grace so that we pray with enthusiasm and earnest faith, properly and without ceasing, for we need to do this; he has asked for it and therefore wants to have it from us. To him be praise, honor, and thanksgiving. Amen."[31]

Chapter 5

Discipline Born of Grace

You probably started this book because you wanted to find a simple way to pray. You have considered Martin Luther's advice to his barber. Using the Lord's Prayer, the Ten Commandments, and the Apostle's Creed as Luther suggests will provide tracks on which your prayer life can run. However, there is more to prayer than this simple method.

The first followers of Jesus were called disciples, meaning "learners" or "pupils," and we are called to be disciples as well. But becoming a disciple of Jesus Christ requires training in spiritual discipline. Paul spoke of this training, this work of discipline, when he wrote, "Exercise yourself toward godliness" (1 Tim. 4:7, ESV).

Donald Whitney, in his book *Spiritual Disciplines for the Christian Life*, defines spiritual disciplines as "God-given means we are to use in the Spirit-filled pursuit of Godliness."[32] We see these means in Luther's life.

Perhaps you noticed, as you read his letter about how to pray, that spiritual disciplines were part of his daily activities. Luther's *The Way to Pray* describes how he invested four hours daily in prayer. A study of his life shows the significant role of the spiritual disciplines of solitude, silence, listening, meditating, journaling, praying, and obeying. These seven elements must be part of our daily discipline if we are to grow in godliness and become like Christ.

As we enter this discussion, we must understand and remember the foundational paradigm of spiritual discipline: God's grace gives us life, and the life we live is our reflection of love for His gift of life to us. We discipline ourselves because this desire is born of grace; it is a Spirit-instilled response of the loving child to do what the Father asks, to become like the Son.

In the course of Luther's life, we can see the wrong way to use discipline and then the right way. Before his conversion, Luther practiced legalistic disciplines in an attempt to gain God's favor. The Reformation grew out of the freedom he found in applying the truth that "the just shall live by faith" (Hab. 2:4; Rom. 1:16; Gal. 3:11; Heb. 10:28).

Roland Bainton, a professor of church history at Princeton Seminary, wrote that, in Luther's time,

"The entire training of home, school, and university was designed to instill fear of God and reverence for the Church."[33] Luther knew the training of very strict discipline that often included physical punishment. He once recalled: "My mother caned me for stealing a nut. . . . My father once whipped me so that I ran away and felt ugly toward him until he was at pains to win me back. And at school I was caned in a single morning fifteen times for nothing at all, I was required to decline and conjugate and hadn't learned my lesson."[34]

As a novice in the Augustinian monastery, Luther's days were filled with strict religious exercises that he was taught would fill his soul with peace. Prayers came seven times daily. After eight hours of sleep, the monks were awakened between 1 and 2 a.m. by the ringing of the cloister bell. Each sprang out of bed, made the sign of the cross, and pulled on the white robe and the scapular, a small cap, without which one was never to leave his cell. Then they spent forty-five minutes in devotion and prayers. Luther's days and nights in the monastery were filled with such exercises for three years.

Luther was told to repent of his sins and do penance. Bainton writes: "Both he attempted to do valiantly, unceasingly. Before long he was conspicuous for his devotedness and scrupulous observations of all the rules of the order. As he himself put it, 'If a monk ever reached heaven by monkery, I would have found my way there also.'"[35]

We can imagine Luther in his cell, a heartsick man crying out as his desperate hands beat his brows, his hungry soul starved his body, and his angry arms whipped his bruised back. He toiled long nights on his knees before the altar and weakened his body with lonely vigils without rest of body or spirit, doing endless penance, ever seeking but never finding peace of mind and soul. Luther would write: "Trouble touches the heart and wakens ardent longing for God's help. No one prays for anything deeply who has not been deeply alarmed."[36]

Luther was desperately seeking God's grace through the physical penance that the Roman Church of his day taught would bring him peace with God. However, the more Luther practiced legalistic physical punishment, self–denial, and self-abasement, the more he realized the depths of his sin and the greatness of his separation from God.

Finally, the Holy Spirit gave Luther new life, and he discovered God's grace (God's riches at Christ's expense). God's gift of grace moved him to a new kind of discipline. A disciplined life of prayer and ministry became his expression of gratitude for all the Father had granted him for Christ's sake.

Heiler would say of Luther in prayer, "Luther is perhaps the most naïve, original, and childlike of the great men of religion, in this realistic desire to influence God."[37] As such, Luther is a good example of the understanding and practice urged by Jesus: "Assuredly, I say to you, whoever does not receive the kingdom of God as a little child will by no means enter it" (Luke 18:17).

Luther came to God as a little child, and so can you. But Luther matured his childlike prayer to that of a spiritual warrior by practicing the spiritual disciplines of solitude, silence, listening, meditating, journaling, praying, and obeying. So now I invite you to add Luther's practice of spiritual disciplines to what you have learned from his *The Way to Pray*.

Solitude

Solitude speaks of an intentional situation that is free from external distraction so that a believer can focus on God with undivided attention. Solitude does not cause God to be present where before He was absent; God is present everywhere (see Ps 139:7–10). However, sin clouds human vision, making it impossible to properly perceive God unless He reveals Himself by His Spirit. A daily meeting in which a believer seeks to behold "the glory of the Lord" transforms

91

him "into the same image from one degree of glory to another. For this comes from the Lord who is the Spirit" (2 Cor. 3:18, ESV). Solitude is where spiritual discipline begins.

Jesus gave very high priority to the practice of solitude. The four Gospels show Jesus practicing solitude of place, solitude of time, and solitude of mind.

First, He practiced solitude of place. This was a battle for Him at times. He was raised in the carpenter's cottage in Nazareth. At least nine people lived under this roof. In addition to Jesus, there were His mother, Mary; Joseph; His four brothers; and at least two sisters. The cottage most likely consisted of a living room, the workshop, and an inner chamber that was a storage closet for provisions, the kitchen utensils, the firewood, etc. he storage closet was a gloomy, secluded place with a latch on the inside. This dark chamber He dedicated to private prayer; it was not less sacred than the cloud-wrapped shrine of the Presence in the temple. He also liked to escape from the house at times.[38]

When Jesus went up to Jerusalem to the feasts, He developed the practice of going to the olive garden of Gethsemane (see Matt. 26:36–46; Mark 14:32–41). Under the branches of some gnarled tree, which was old when Isaiah was young, our Lord must have watched the stars through many summer nights.

When our Lord entered on His public ministry, finding solitude became even more difficult. Jesus was frequently entertained by those who showed Him little courtesy and provided Him no place of privacy. Therefore, Jesus would frequently withdraw from the towns "to desolate places and pray" (Luke 5:16, ESV). When His spirit hungered for communion with His Father, He dismissed the crowds and "went up on the mountain by himself to pray. When evening came, he was there alone" (Matt. 14:22–23, ESV). When He perceived that "they were about to come and take him by force to make him king, Jesus withdrew again to the mountain by himself" (John 6:15, ESV). The solitary place Jesus seemed to like most was the mountains. In the mountains, there is more than simple solitude to assist prayer; there is a ministry of creation that soothes the mind and moves it to worship the Creator:

> *Cold mountains and the midnight air*
> *Witnessed the fervor of His prayer.*[39]

Jesus also practiced solitude of time. We are told that on at least one occasion, He rose *"very early in the morning*, while it was still dark, . . . departed and went out to a desolate place, and there he prayed

(Mark 1:35, ESV, emphasis added). Often Jesus spent extended time alone in prayer; for example, the night before He selected the Twelve and called them apostles, "He went out to the mountain to pray, and continued all night in prayer to God" (Luke 6:12).

Jesus also had solitude of mind. Often the crowds surrounded Jesus and pressed in on Him (see Luke 8:45; John 6:15). In spite of the throngs, Jesus said, "I am not alone, for the Father is with me" (John 16:32; see also John 8:29; 14:10).

If you want to be alone with God, you must choose to be alone. Take yourself away from the busyness of doing things and the distraction of talking with others. Think in terms of the right place or the right time; consistent use of these for solitude will enable you to enjoy meaningful conversation with God in prayer if you focus on Him alone.

Getting alone with God in prayer does not contradict the practice of praying with other believers. Jesus said that when two on earth are at one about something for which they pray, it shall be done for them (see Matt. 18:19). Commenting on these words of Jesus, Luther said: "How much more should they obtain that for which they pray when a whole city comes together unitedly to praise or to pray. . . . We can and we ought, indeed, to pray in all places and at all times; but prayer is nowhere so vigorous and so strong as when a great number pray in unison."[40]

Luther recognized the importance of prayer with other believers, but he built his daily schedule around his time alone with the Lord. He saw this time of solitude as significant not only for each day but he also used this time to prepare for his inevitable experience of solitude at death. One day as he talked about prayer, Luther said: "The confrontation with death and its demands comes to us all; no one can die for another. All must fight their own battle with death by themselves, alone. I will not be with you then, nor you with me."

On February 18, 1547, about 3 a.m., Luther died in the city of his birth, Eisleben. Surrounded by witnesses, Justus Jonas, Luther's longtime confidant, shook the dying man by the arm to rouse his spirit for the final exertion. "Reverend father, will you die steadfast in Christ and the doctrines you have preached?" "Yes," replied the clear voice for the last time.[41] Those who follow Luther's example of beginning each day with a time of solitude with the Savior will be more able to be alone with Christ as they face death.

Your battle for solitude can be won through prayer. Ask the Lord to enable you to properly find and use solitude. Ask Him to guide you to find the right place and the right time to meet with Him. In some situations, neither a place nor a time for solitude can be found; but if you are consistent in using solitude, you can learn to clothe your soul in divine quietness even in the crowded marketplace.

Silence

> *God comes to me in silent hours,*
> *As morning dew to summer flowers.*[42]

If solitude means getting away from the busyness *around* us, silence is stilling the busyness *within* us. Before we talk with God, we want to free ourselves from internal distractions. Scripture says, "Be silent in the presence of the Lord GOD; for the day of the LORD is at hand, for the LORD has prepared a sacrifice; He has invited His guests" (Zeph. 1:7), and "Be still and know that I am God" (Ps. 46:10).

Amy Carmichael knew a strength that she found alone with God in prayer. Her father died when she was eighteen, and she spent fifty-six years in India rescuing children who had been temple prostitutes. In her thirty-five published works, we can see a woman who knew God and His love in her life. Amy insisted:

Do not be afraid of silence in your prayer time.

It may be that you are meant to listen, not to speak. So wait before the Lord. Wait in stillness. Wait as David waited when he "sat before the Lord." And in that stillness, assurance will come to you. You will know that you are heard; you will know that your Lord ponders the voice of your humble desires; you will hear quiet words spoken to you yourself, perhaps to your surprise and refreshment.[43]

It seems to be a natural tendency for us, when in solitude, to spend all our time filling the silence with talking, but we need silence if we would listen to God speaking to us.

Dietrich Bonhoeffer said, "The Word comes not to the chatterer but to him who holds his tongue."[44] Francois Fenelon observed, "Oh how rare it is to find a soul quiet enough to hear God speak!"[45]

Luther recommended what we commonly call sentence prayers, succinctly saying what you mean to say in numerous but short prayers. He insisted that those who wish to pray properly should say "brief prayers" that are "pregnant with spirit, strongly fortified by faith."[46] Luther declared: "The fewer the words, the better the prayer. The more the words, the worse the prayer. Few words and much meaning is Christian. Many words and little meaning is pagan."[47]

Jesus said it in this way: "But when you pray, do not use vain repetitions, as the heathen do: for they think that they shall be heard for their much speaking" (Matt. 6:7).

The spiritual discipline of silence is saying simply what you mean to say to God, then ceasing to speak so that you can listen to Him.

Listening

When you find solitude, away from the busyness of life, and still your heart in silence, then you are best prepared for prayer, for conversation with God.

When you talk with Him, how do you know what to ask for? James, a disciple and half-brother of our Lord, said, "You ask and do not receive, because you ask amiss, that you may spend it on your pleasures" (James 4:3). Eugene Peterson paraphrased what James wrote, saying: "You wouldn't think of just asking God for it, would you? And why not? Because you know you'd be asking for what you have no right to. You're spoiled children, each wanting your own way" (James 4:3, *Message*).

How can we listen to God so that we can ask Him to meet our needs in His way? We turn to the Bible, as Luther did in the Lord's Prayer and the Ten Commandments, and see how God shows us the right motives for prayer and what to pray for. As we meditate on His Word, the first thing we may discover is that we must be truly willing to listen to Him.

George Mueller, a man who turned in prayer to God alone to supply the needs of His children, and whom God supplied with more than $7.5 million to care for 120,000 orphans in nineteenth-century England, is best and rightly known for his long and fruitful prayer life. To explain his approach to God, he wrote:

> I seek at the beginning to get my heart into such a state that it has no will of its own in regard to a given matter. Nine-tenths of the difficulties are overcome when our hearts are ready to do the Lord's will, whatever it may be. Having done this, I do not leave the result to feeling or simple impression. If I do so, I make myself liable to a great delusion. I seek the will of the Spirit of God through, or in connection with the Word of God. The Spirit and the Word must be combined. If I look to the Spirit alone, without the Word, I lay myself open to great

delusions also. If the Holy Spirit guides us at all, He will do it according to the Scriptures, and never contrary to them. Next I take into account providential circumstances. I ask God in prayer to reveal to me his will aright. Thus through prayer to God, the study of the Word, and reflection, I come to a deliberate judgment according to the best of my knowledge and ability, and, if my mind is thus at peace, I proceed accordingly.[48]

The will of God is revealed as you listen to the Spirit of God in the Word of God. The precepts and promises of the Bible teach us *what* to pray. They teach us what grace to ask for and for what work we need strength. On every page of the Bible there is subject matter for prayer. B. F. Westcott, a renowned nineteenth-century English Bible scholar, observed: "The petitions of true disciples are echoes (so to speak) of Christ's words. As He has spoken so they speak. Their prayer is only some fragment of His teaching transformed into a supplication, and so it will necessarily be heard."[49]

One way to pray more effectively is to echo God's Word back to Him as you pray. We align our hearts with His heart as we pray His Words from our hearts.

The most significant example of this kind of an echo prayer was given by our Lord as He died on the cross. Three of the seven last recorded statements of Christ are prayers. We have seen that two of these prayers were *echoes* of Scripture. Christ, the Living Word, was so saturated with the written Word that in His most painful moments, as He faced death and separation from His Father, He instinctively cried out in the words of Scripture.

Thomas Cobbet also sees prayer as an *echo*. Cobbet alludes to Paul's words in Romans 8:26–27 when he calls prayer "the harmonious, sweet-sounding echo of the Spirit, who speaks first to the heart."[50] If we would hear the Spirit speak, we must listen.

We see again from Stoltz that "Christian prayer is a spiritual echo; it is God's voice sounding in the human heart and resounding up to heaven from whence it comes."[51] Likewise, Manikha Vacagar says, "The tongue itself, which cries to Thee, nay all the powers of my being which cry to Thee—all are thine."[52] Christians down through the ages have turned to God's Word to understand His heart and to listen for His will for them in prayer.[53]

If your prayer would echo God's voice speaking to your heart, then you must listen to Him through His Word before you speak in prayer. In fact, listening is the basis of asking; only listening can make prayer align with His will. In prayer, we should not presume to tell God what to do; we need to find out what He wants us to do. Thus, from our side, prayer begins in listening to the Word of God.

John Owen, a seventeenth-century English pastor who spoke before Parliament and served both Oliver Cromwell and King Charles, wrote, "We are to pray only for what God has promised, and the communication of it unto us in that way whereby He will work it and affect it."[54] John Calvin, the leader of the Reformation in Switzerland, warned, "Their presumption is great who rush into the presence of God without call from His Word."[55]

A current Scottish theologian, Sinclair Ferguson, has said: "The promise which God gives creates the objective possibility of prayer, while the Spirit (who is Himself given within the scope of the divine promises) is the condition of its subjective realization. His work is vital since prayer (in contrast to the doctrine of prayer) is *a gift, ability or spiritual faculty*."[56] As we meditate on God's Word, His Spirit helps us.

Writing to the first-century church in Rome, Paul explains how the Spirit helps us as we pray: "Likewise the Spirit also helps in our weaknesses. For we do not know what we should pray for as we ought, but the Spirit Himself makes intercession for us with groanings which cannot be uttered. Now He who searches the hearts knows what the mind of the Spirit is, because He makes intercession for the saints according to the will of God" (Rom. 8:26–27).

The Holy Spirit is "the Spirit of grace and supplication" (Zech. 12:10) who helps us when we pray. His help is available in both the matter and the manner of our praying if we will listen to His voice. Jesus promised, "If you abide in Me, and My words abide in you, you will ask what you desire, and it shall be done for you" (John 15:7).

Meditation

When you pray, you come to God in solitude and you quiet your heart in silence to listen to His Word. Meditation is the mother of devotion and the daughter of solitude. Meditating on Scripture turns the written Word of the Bible into the living Word of your soul. In solitude, you meditate on the Word to understand how it applies to your life today. You find God in His Word, ready to guide your heart and life. Then you know how to approach Him in prayer.

Meditating on the Bible means that you regard its words as nourishing food. With your mind and your heart, you *chew* the words of God well as you consider them from many angles. You *digest* them as you understand and welcome the truth into your life. You regard them as essential to your soul's well-being. In meditation, you engage all the faculties of your soul—your mind, emotion, will, and spirit—focusing on the Lord with your whole being so that you can follow Him with your whole being.

The psalmist wrote: "I will meditate on Your precepts, and contemplate Your ways. . . . My eyes are awake through the night watches, that I may meditate on Your word. Hear my voice according to Your loving-kindness; O LORD, revive me according to Your justice" (Ps 119:15,148–149).

The Hebrew word translated "meditate" also means "to mutter" or "to utter." Sometimes this word is translated as the English word *speak*, as in "My tongue shall *speak* of Your righteousness and of Your praise all the day long" (Ps. 35:28). When the psalmist said, "His delight is in the law of the LORD, and on His law he meditates day and night" (Ps. 1:2), he meant that he audibly recited the law of God and spoke his reflections on the law *aloud*. And when the psalmist wrote, "I will also meditate on all Your works; I muse on the work of Your hands" (Ps. 77:12) and "I remember the days of long ago; I meditate on all Your works and consider what Your hands have done" (Ps. 143:5), he meant he *audibly* listed God's works. He thought out loud as he considered what God's hands had done. As you meditate, speak out loud; you will find that it stimulates thought and helps your mind engage and focus.

The prophet Isaiah wrote:

> This is what the LORD says to me:
> "As a lion growls,
> a great lion over his prey—
> and though a whole band of shepherds
> is called together against him,
> he is not frightened by their shouts
> or disturbed by their clamor—
> so the LORD Almighty will come down
> to do battle on Mount Zion and on its
> heights." (Isaiah 31:4, NIV)

When you meditate on God's promises, you should be like a hungry lion growling over his freshly taken prey, one who will not be distracted by anything, ready for the Lord to come down and do battle for you. Do not let the noise, hurry, and crowds fluster you.

Biblical mediation is not the same as Zen, Yoga, or Transcendental Meditation. These practices seek to empty the mind. Christian meditation is emptying the mind of temporal concerns and filling it with God's

Word. Transcendental Meditation sees meditation as a way to control brain waves in order to improve psychological and emotional well-being. Christian meditation does not need or expect any special gifts or psychic powers. Bernard of Clairvaux explained, "Waiting on God is not idleness but work which beats all other work to one unskilled in it."[57]

The best preparation for meditation is recognizing its importance and being prepared to learn and grow through a staunch determination to persevere in its practice. The spiritual discipline of meditation on God's Word will enrich your understanding of His heart and His ways for your life. Through it, you can hear His Word give you direction for prayer.

Journaling

Reading makes a full man,
Writing an exact man.[58]

You find a place away from interruptions, a place of solitude, alone with God. You still the noise of thoughts that parade through your mind and come in silence to God's Word. You listen to what God's Word says. You meditate on His Word, not only reading it, but taking time to absorb its meaning for your life. In every step of this process, you ask God to help you and meet you where you are. You ask

Him to advance His kingdom in your heart and with your life.

But how do you remember how He leads you and what He shows you to ask for in prayer? You write it down in a journal, recording these events of your journey with God in prayer.

God Himself did not rely on human memory to pass His Word from generation to generation—He inspired His Word to be written so there could be precise understanding of His truth. Many psalms are examples of journaling, as David was inspired by the Holy Spirit to leave us an example of his journey with God in prayer. In the book of Lamentations, Jeremiah's journal reveals what God inspired him to record for us of his thoughts and feelings about the fall of Jerusalem.

Whitney enumerates eight values of journaling:

1. It helps our self-understanding.
2. It helps in meditation.
3. It helps in expressing thoughts and feelings to the Lord.
4. It helps in remembering the Lord's works.
5. It helps in creating and preserving a spiritual heritage.
6. It helps in clarifying and articulating insights

107

and impressions.

7. It helps in monitoring goals and priorities.
8. It helps in maintaining the other spiritual disciplines.[59]

In his prayer journal, Mueller left his son a legacy of more than fifty thousand answered prayers.

How do you keep a journal? You may want to read a book by or about someone who has kept a spiritual journal, but I would encourage you to start by writing your thoughts and feelings as you meditate and God shows you how to pray. Look at the eight values of journaling previously listed for ideas of what you may want to include. You will soon develop your own style of recording what you most want to remember.

Prayer

You are with God, in solitude and silence. You listen to Him speak to you through His Word and meditate on it to understand His direction for your life. You record in your journal His Word for you and how He leads you to pray to Him. You have prepared your heart for prayer.

As you practice the spiritual discipline of prayer, you will find that the various characteristics of God motivate distinctive types of prayer. Awareness of

God's greatness stimulates us to *adoration*, praising Him in prayer. Adoring God's divine perfections, changes believers into the same image, from glory to glory Realization of His righteousness reveals our sinfulness and moves us to *confession*, asking God for forgiveness of sins, confessing our sins, deepens the sense of sin. Recognizing God's justice reveals the undeniable guilt of the human race and the necessity of divine punishment which leads believers to *lamentation*, expressing sorrow. Consciousness of God's grace and goodness inspires us to *thanksgiving*, thanking Him for what He has done. Rendering thanks enlivens gratitude. Knowledge of God's mighty power and of specific human need stirs us to *supplication*, coming to God with our requests. When requests are for our own needs, we come to God with *petition*. When requests are for the needs of others, we come to God in *intercession*. We bring all these are kinds of prayers to our Almighty God, knowing that He hears us and will answer when we pray.

The practice of prayer may raise a number of practical questions. Let's consider five of these questions:

Must we use words in prayer?
Words are the normal vehicle of communicating with God in prayer. Jesus' Pattern Prayer and His High Priestly Prayer were spoken and written. The book of Psalms contains 150 written prayers. The

epistles of the apostle Paul are filled with his written prayers.

While words are the normal vehicle for communicating with God, sometimes words are inadequate. Rabbis speaking of the power of the spoken word in prayer claim that tears are more powerful than words (see 2 Kings 20:5; Psalm 39:12; 56:8). Jesus prayed "with loud cries and tears" (Heb 5:7, ESV). In Gethsemane, Christ's bloody sweat was the most powerful of all prayers. And some life situations are so intense that even God the Holy Spirit cannot find words; He can only groan (see Rom. 8:26). It should not surprise us, therefore, that mere humans are sometimes at a loss for words when they pray.

When this happens to you, take heart; God the Holy Spirit intercedes "for us with groanings which cannot be uttered," and when He does, God the Father hears and answers.

If we use words, should they be many or few?

The number of words you use depends on what you need to say. Jesus taught His followers: "When you pray, do not keep on babbling like pagans, for they think they will be heard because of their many words. Do not be like them, for your Father knows what you need before you ask him. This, then, is how you should pray: 'Our Father in heaven . . .'"

(Matt. 6:7–9, NIV). The Pattern Prayer that follows this instruction contains only fifty-seven words in the original Greek. David explains that God is near to all who "call on him in truth" (Ps. 145:18, NIV). The challenge is to earnestly speak truth from the heart. Believers should heed Soloman's counsel; "Be not rash with your mouth, nor let your heart be hasty to utter a word before God, for God is in heaven and you are on earth. Therefore let your words be few" (Eccl. 5:2, ESV).

Should prayer be audible or silent?

Christ is our pattern, and in Gethsemane He prayed aloud. God knows our thoughts, which means that He hears silent prayer, but praying aloud can help keep our minds focused. Pray aloud when you can, but know that God hears words spoken in your heart to Him.

Some situations are so hostile to the faith that audible prayer is not possible. For example, when Geoffrey Bull was a missionary in a Tibetan prison, he was not permitted to utter any audible prayer.

Some needs are so intense they we just don't know how to express them in words. Groans and sighs may be all that can be uttered. Hannah so desired a child that she "was speaking in her heart, and her lips were moving, but her voice was not heard"

(1 Sam. 1:13, NASB). In Romans 8:26, Paul reminds us that "We do not know how we ought to pray, but the Spirit himself intercedes for us with groans that words cannot express."

Of course, without speaking, we cannot share prayer with others so that they can hear and agree with us. Abraham Kuyper, who at the turn of the twentieth century developed his foundational concepts of Christian worldview, said: "Prayer without words rarely satisfies the soul. Mere mental prayer is necessarily imperfect; earnest, fervent prayer constrains us to express it in words."[60]

Is it proper to pray prayers written by others?
Recited prayers are useful to keep us in touch with sound doctrine that has stood the test of time and practice. Left to ourselves, we could easily slip away from "the faith once given" (Jude 1:3) into a phantom of *our own religion*. Recited prayers remind us of things we ought to ask, especially when we are praying for others. Urgent matters can fill spontaneous prayer, while important matters may then be left out. If we speak only in spontaneous prayer, there is danger that important, great, permanent, and objective necessities may get crowded out or unintentionally omitted.

C. S. Lewis, a twentieth-century English professor,

writer, and Christian philosopher, gave the best usage of recited prayers when he said: "It does not matter very much who first put them together. If they are our own words they will soon, by unavoidable repetition, harden into a formula. If they are someone else's, we shall continually pour into them our own meaning."[61] The *Book of Common Prayer* and *The Puritan Hope* are two collections of prayers that have stood the test of time and which you may use with great benefit.

Must prayers be expressed in eloquent words?

If the word *eloquent* is taken to mean expressive and carefully chosen words, this type of prayer shows earnestness and sincerity, and is to be commended. But when we speak of eloquence in prayer, we usually mean high-sounding and flowery speech that is used to impress its hearers. This is one of the greatest of all abominations.

When Jesus gave His disciples what we call the Lord's Prayer, He said: "In this manner, therefore, pray" (Matt. 6:9). This was His pattern for His disciples, and it is the pattern for us, as well. We have already discussed at length Luther's example in this regard. To merely recite Scripture or other prayers that have not flowed through the mind, the heart, and the will reduces prayer to the level of a parrot's chatter. Christ's object was to furnish His disciples with basic truths on the subject of prayer. He did not mean to limit His church to these words. Our Savior gave His disciples this prayer, not as words with magical powers, but as a pattern for sincere expression and an example in substance and manner.

Obedience

In solitude, silence, and meditation you seek God's Word and His direction for you, and your journal records this. In prayer, you commune with God, seeking to be conformed to the Son, and you are prepared to confront the evil that would defeat you.

In the final analysis, how is the soundness of prayer measured? Our prayers must be fervent, but passion alone is not enough to make prayer effective. Our words are important, but striving for eloquence in prayer to puff up our own importance offends God. Words spoken from the lips alone and not from the heart, like outward deeds performed without a true intention of the heart, are vain. In a word, once we have prayed, we must obey.

The writer of Proverbs explained: "Like a coating of glaze over earthenware are fervent lips with an evil heart. A malicious man disguises himself with his lips, but in his heart he harbors deceit" (Prov. 26:23–24, NIV).

The Talmud contains authoritative teaching of the ancient Jewish rabbis. It declares, "God hates him who speaks one way with the heart and another way with the mouth." This divorce of heart from behavior is hypocrisy. Hypocrisy corrupts the conscience. It tells me that I can say one thing and do another, and that is all right. Our Lord calls us to holiness and love, and these are heart attitudes displayed in our actions. In Matthew 15, we see that Jesus was so bold in His denunciation of the hypocrisy of the Pharisees that His disciples were concerned that Jesus had offended them. Jesus wasn't concerned about offending the Pharisees, but about honoring God from the heart.

In the final analysis, the soundness of prayer is measured by our behavior after we have prayed. We simply must obey. As John Bunyan said, "You can do no more than pray before you pray, but you cannot do more than pray until you have prayed."

Herbert Lockyer, in *All the Prayers of the Bible*, explained: "Three requirements for prevailing intercessory prayer are: 1. A desire for the highest spiritual and material interests of those prayed for. 2. The utmost confidence in the divine promise and sufficiency to meet the need. 3. Readiness to cooperate in action as an outcome of intercession."[62]

Genuine intercession always requires that we place ourselves, with all our means and our energies, at God's disposal for His purposes of grace toward those for whom we pray. Intercession thus leads up to and requires complete dedication.

In the Hebrew Bible, the word translated "to hear" literally means "to obey." Thus, obedience signifies an active response to something one has heard, rather than passive listening. To hear God's Word means to obey that Word. "Now if you obey me fully [really hear me] and keep my covenant, then out of all nations you will be my treasured possession. Although the whole earth is mine, you will be for me a kingdom of priests and a holy nation" (Ex. 19:5–6, NIV; literal meaning in brackets). One cannot *truly* hear God's word without acting on it.

Obedience is the supreme test of faith in God and reverence for Him. Samuel said: "Does the LORD delight in burnt offerings and sacrifices as much as in obeying the voice of the LORD? To obey is better than sacrifice, and to heed is better than the fat of rams" (1 Sam. 15:22, NIV).

No one can sustain a right relationship with the Lord without obedience. Every thought must be made captive to and obedient to Christ (see 2 Cor. 10:5). Nothing less than wholehearted obedience to the truth is acceptable to God (Rom. 6:17).

Matthew recorded that Jesus exclaimed: "I praise you, Father, Lord of heaven and earth, because you have hidden these things from the wise and learned, and revealed them to little children" (Matt. 11:2). Oswald Chambers, author of the Christian classic *My Utmost for His Highest*, shared the following thoughts on this verse:

> All God's revelations are sealed until they are opened to us by obedience. You will never get them open by philosophy and thinking. Immediately you obey, a flash of light comes. Let God's truth work in you by soaking in it, not by worrying into it. The only way you can get to know it is to stop trying to find out and by being born again. Obey God in the thing He shows you, and immediately the next thing is opened up. One reads tomes on the work of the Holy Spirit, when one five minutes of drastic obedience would make things as clear as a sunbeam. "I suppose I shall understand these things some day!" You can understand them now. It is not study that does it, but obedience. The tiniest fragment of obedience and heaven opens up and the profoundest truths of God

are yours straight away. God will never reveal more truth about Himself until you have obeyed what you know already.[63]

We must obey what God asks us to do if we would continue to hear His voice. And we must persevere in prayer. In Luke 11, Jesus spoke of persistence in prayer in His parable about the man who gave his friend what he needed. Luther responded to Jesus' urging with these words:

We should never lose heart; but we should persist in praying, wishing, and seeking until hope and the awaited liberation appear.[64]

There is no Christian who does not have time to pray without ceasing. By that, I mean spiritual praying. No one is so heavily burdened with his labor, that if he will, he can, while working, speak with God in his heart, lay before him his need and that of other men, ask for help, make petition, and all this exercise strengthen his faith.[65]

With passionate zeal, Luther exclaimed: "One should not only pray for an hour, but one must cry out and knock; you must forthwith compel God to come. As God continues to hide Himself, so begin to knock, and cease not until you have burst open the door which encloses Him. Audacious prayer, which perseveres unflinchingly and ceases not through fear, is well pleasing unto God."

As you continue to come to God in solitude and silence, to meditate on His Word and listen to His voice, you will record an amazing story in your journal. It will be an exciting journey with God, and someday you will look back with so many of the saints whose words you have considered in this book to marvel that God would allow us to have a part in His kingdom, a part that He gives us as we come to Him in a simple way to pray.

Conclusion

Thank you for reading *A Simple Way to Pray*. I hope you have enjoyed it and I pray that it will help you grow in your knowledge, understanding, and practice of prayer. Martin Luther's passion for prayer grew out of his passion for God, and I hope that same passion for God has stirred within you as you have read this book.

For the first thirty years of my ministry, I had the privilege to serve God in many roles. I pastored churches in Massachusetts, Alabama, Maryland, and Florida. I served as the international director of Evangelism Explosion for thirteen years and authored a number of publications. I also served on the board of directors for Ligonier Ministries and Mission America. In 1982, I launched Serve International, an equipping ministry focused on training believers in relational evangelism.

During all these years, I prayed, but I had little passion

for prayer. Then, in 1993, God began instilling in me a new passion for prayer. As the coordinator for church vitality with Mission to North America, the church-planting arm of the Presbyterian Church in America, I worked for more than ten years developing and refining the equipping of Kingdom Intercessors.

The directors of Serve International and I have a vision of preparing believers for spiritual warfare and revival by instilling passion for Kingdom-focused Prayer and equipping an army of 120 Kingdom Intercessors in 120 churches in 120 cities and regions—1,728,000 people—to invest about an hour a day praying for their hearts, homes, churches, and personal worlds. This will be accomplished as we equip individuals in Kingdom-focused Prayer discipleship.

Over the past fifteen years, as the Holy Spirit instilled in me an increasing passion for Kingdom-focused Prayer, I recorded in my journal the lessons He taught me. I also noted insights I gained from great people of prayer. When I shared these materials with other believers, many of them urged me to make them available on a broader basis. So these materials are now being professionally edited and made available to others.

Our Lord Jesus Christ commands us to pray, and we must obey. In prayer, we communicate with the God of the universe who loves us so very much. I pray that the Spirit of grace and supplication will instill in you a growing passion for Kingdom-focused Prayer. Will you join me in asking the Lord of hosts to raise a vast army of mighty prayer warriors?

May God bless you,

Archie

Endnotes

1 Friedrich Heiler, *Prayer: A Study in the History and Psychology of Religion* (London: Oxford University Press, 1932), 130.

2 Helmut Thieliche, *The Waiting Father* (London: James Clarke & Co., 1939), 65.

3 Roland H. Bainton, *Here I Stand: A Life of Martin Luther* (New York: Meridian, div. of Penguin Books, 1977), 34

4 William Stevenson, *The Story of the Reformation* (Richmond, Va.: John Knox Press, 1959), 30–31. Also see Heiko Oberman, *Luther: Man Between God and the Devil* (New York: Image Books, Doubleday, 1989), 92

5 Heiler, *Prayer,* 262.

6 "A Mighty Fortress is Our God" has been called the "Battle Hymn of the Reformation" for the effect it had in increasing the support for the Reformers' cause. John Julian records four theories of its origin (*A Dictionary of Hymnology: Setting forth the Origin and History of Christian Hymns of all Ages and Nations,* 2nd revised edition, 2 vols., n.p., 1907). It was written sometime between 1527 and 1529. Ironically, this hymn is now suggested for Catholic masses, appearing in the second edition of the Catholic Book of Worship, published by the Canadian Conference of Catholic Bishops.

7 *Psalter Hymnal, Centennial Edition* (Grand Rapids, Mich.: Publication Committee of the Christian Reformed Church, 1959), 516–517.

8 Oberman, *Luther: Man Between God and the* Devil, 38–39.

9 Bainton, *Here I* Stand, 144.

10 Ibid.

11 Heiler, *Prayer,* 118.

12 Ibid., 281.

13 Karl Barth, *Prayer According to the Catechism of the Reformation* (Philadelphia: Westminster Press, 1952), 9.

14 Heiler, *Prayer,* xiii.

15 Carl J. Schindler, "Introduction," "A Simple Way to Pray," in *Luther's Works,* American Edition, Vol. 43, Devotional Writings, Vol. II, trans. Carl J. Schindler, ed. Gustav K. Wiencke (Minneapolis: Fortress Press, 1968), 189.

16 Ibid., 119.

17 Ibid., 231.

18 J. Pelikan, ed., *Luther's Works*, Vol. 6 (St. Louis, Mo.: Concordia, 1955), 159.

19 Moses said there were *ten words* in reference to the Ten Commandments (See Exodus 34:28; Deuteronomy 4:13; 10:4), but there is difference of opinion as to how these commands are to be numbered. Josephus is the first witness for the division now common among Protestants (except Lutherans) as: 1. Foreign gods, 2. Images, 3. Name of God, 4. Sabbath, 5. Parents, 6. Murder, 7. Adultery, 8. Theft, 9. False witness, 10. Coveting. Augustine combined foreign gods and images (see Exodus 20:2–6) into one and following the order of Deuteronomy 5:21 made the ninth commandment a prohibition of coveting a neighbor's wife, while the tenth prohibits the coveting of house and other property. Roman Catholics and Lutherans accept Augustine's mode of reckoning, except that they follow the order of Exodus 20:17, so that the ninth commandment forbids the coveting of a neighbor's house, while the tenth includes his wife and property. The prohibition of images which is introduced by the solemn formula "you shall not" is surely a different *word* from the command to worship no other gods than Jehovah. Moreover, if nine of the ten words were commandments, it would seem reasonable to make the remaining *word* a commandment, if this can be done without violence to the subject matter. ("The Ten Commandments," in International Bible Encyclopedia, Vol. 5 [Grand Rapids, Mich.: Eerdmans, 1952], 2944–2947.)

20 Since Luther combined commands one and two as other Protestants see them, this additional information on carved images has been added. This is a composite of thoughts from *Luther's Small Catechism*, the Heidelberg Catechism, and the Westminster Shorter Catechism.

21 Ibid., 246.

22 Ibid.,251.

23 Martin Luther, foreword to the Neuburg edition of the Psalter (n.p., 1545).

24 Ibid.

25 Ibid.

26 From Martin Luther's hymn "A Mighty Fortress Is Our God."

27 W. Stanford Reid, "The Battle Hymns of the Lord—Calvinist Psalmody of the Sixteenth Century," *Sixteenth Century Journal* 2/1 (1971): 36–37.

28 Dietrich Bonhoeffer, "Life Together and The Prayer Book of the Bible," *Works*, Vol. 5 (Minneapolis: Fortress Press, 1996), 54.

29 Ibid., 45–47.

30 Ibid., 157.

31 Luther, foreword to the Neuburg edition of the Psalter.

32 Donald Whitney, *Spiritual Disciplines for the Christian Life* (Colorado Springs, Colo.: NavPress, 1991), 17.

33 Bainton, *Here I Stand*, 20.

34 Ibid, 17.

35 Ibid, 34.

36 Heiler, *Prayer,* 231.

37 Heiler, *Prayer*, 131.

38 James Stalker, "Christ As A Man of Prayer," in *Imago Christi: The Example of Jesus Christ* (New York: American Tract Society, 1889), 126–144.

39 From the hymn "My Dear Redeemer and My Lord." Cited in David M'Intyre, *The Hidden Life of Prayer* (Pensacola: Mt. Zion Bible Church, n.d.), 16.

40 Heiler, *Prayer*, 238.

41 Oberman, *Martin Luther: Man Between God and the Devil*, 3

42 Attributed to Mechthild von Magdeburg.

43 Amy Carmichael, *Thou Givest. . . . They Gather* (London Lutterworth Press, 1959), 43.

44 Bonhoeffer, "Life Together and The Prayer Book of the Bible."

45 Heiler, *Prayer*.

46 J. Pelikan, ed., *Luther's Works*, Vol. 30 (St. Louis, Mo.: Concordia, 1955), 322.

47 Gerhard Ebeling, *On Prayer*, trans. James Leitch (Philadelphia Fortress Press, 1966), 47.

48 Heiler, *Prayer*, 439–440.

49 B. F. Westcott, *The Gospel According to St. John* (Grand Rapids, Mich.: Eerdmans, n.d.), 218.

50 Heiler, *Prayer*, 114.

51 Ibid.

52 Ibid.

53 Ibid.

54 John Owen, cited in Sinclair Ferguson, *John Owen on the Christian Life* (Edinburgh: Banner of Truth Trust, 1987), 271.

55 Heiler, *Prayer*, 114.

56 Owen, cited in Ferguson, *John Owen on the Christian Life*, 271.

57 Heiler, *Prayer*.

58 Attributed to Sir Francis Bacon.

59 Whitney, *Spiritual Disciplines for the Christian Life*, 14.

60 Abraham Kuyper, *The Person and the Work of the Holy Spirit* (Grand Rapids: Zondervan, 1956), 623.

61 C. S. Lewis, *Letters to Malcolm: Chiefly on Prayer* (San Diego Harvest, HBJ, 1964), 11–12.

62 Herbert Lockyer, *All the Prayers of the Bible* (Grand Rapids Zondervan, 1959), 189.

63 Oswald Chambers, *My Utmost for His Highest* (New York Dodd, Mead and Co., 1954), 284.

64 J. Pelikan, ed., *Luther's Works*, Vol. 5 (St. Louis, Mo. Concordia, 1955), 362.

65 Hugh Thomas Kerr, Jr., ed., *A Compendia of Luther's Theology* (Philadelphia: Westminster Press, 1943), 109.

Bibliography

Bainton, Roland H. *Here I Stand: The Life of Martin Luther.* New York: Meridian, a div. of Penguin Books, 1977.

Bonhoeffer, Dietrich. "Life Together and The Prayer Book of the Bible." *Works*, Vol. 5. Minneapolis, Minn.: Fortress Press, 1996.

Brokering, Herbert F., ed. *Luther's Prayers.* Augsburg Fortress Press, Minneapolis, 1994.

Burns, James MacGregor. "Revolutionary Leadership." *Leadership.* New York: Harper & Row, 1978.

Heiler, Friedrich. *Prayer, A Study in the History and Psychology of Religion.* London: Oxford University Press, 1932.

Luther, Martin. *Luther's Small Catechism with Explanations.* St. Louis: Concordia Publishing House, 1986.

_____. "A Simple Way to Pray." *Luther's Works*, American Edition, Vol. 43, Devotional Writings, Vol. II, trans. Carl J. Schindler, ed. Gustav K. Wiencke. Minneapolis: Fortress Press, 1968.

_____. *The Larger Catechism of Martin Luther.* Philadelphia, Fortress Press, 1959.

_____. *Luther's Works*, 55 vol. set. Gen ed. Jaroslav Pelikan (vols. 1–30) and Helmut T. Lehmann (vols. 31–55). Philadelphia: Fortress Press, 1968.

_____. *Luther's Works,* CD-ROM. Ed. Jaroslav Pelikan ;gen. ed. Helmut T. Lehmann. Philadelphia: Fortress Press, 2001.

MacCulloch, Diarmaid. "Luther: A Good Monk, 1483–1517." *The Reformation.* New York: Viking Penguin Group, 2003.

Mosheim, John Lawrence Von, *Institutes of Ecclesiastical History, Ancient and Modern,* New York, Thomas N. Stanford, Church Publishing House, 1857,

Oberman, Heiko. *Luther: Man Between God and the Devil.* New York: Image Books, Doubleday, 1989.

Stevenson, William. The Story of the Reformation, Richmond, Va.: John Knox Press, 1959.

Scripture Index

Serve International

Serving Believers and Churches through Kingdom-Focused Prayer

Jesus commanded, "Seek first the kingdom of God," and He taught us to pray, "Your kingdom come." These words need to be taken very seriously. The American culture is collapsing because most of our churches are powerless, and most of the churches are powerless because they are prayerless. Jesus said, "My house shall be a called a house of prayer for all nations."

God is using Serve International's Kingdom Intercessors' Training to provide believers and local church leaders with the vision, training, and tools to equip others to pray with greater power.

Serve International's mission is to help believers participate with Jesus in His ministry of intercession by *igniting* their passion for Kingdom-focused Prayer and *equipping* them to pray with kingdom focus so they can effectively engage in spiritual warfare, help to revitalize their local churches so that they become "houses of prayer for all nations" (Isa. 56:7; Mark 11:17), and prepare for revival by 120^3.

Serve International's vision is 120 to the third power (120^3). Inspired by the incident recorded in Acts 1:12–2:47, when about 120 men and women engaged in extraordinary prayer and God brought the outpouring of the Holy Spirit at Pentecost, we will plead with the Lord to revive His people in the North American church. Specifically, we will plead with God until He develops a supercritical mass of Kingdom-focused Prayer, through a network of 120 Kingdom Intercessors in 120 local churches networked organically in 120 cities, regions, or areas in the countries of North America.

Serve International, a 501c3 nonprofit organization, ministers to a wide range of evangelical churches of varying sizes. Serve is funded by gifts from those who share our heart for the revival of the church and expansion of God's kingdom.

You may send your gift by mail to

Serve International
PO Box 71716
Marietta, GA 30007

You may contribute online at:

www.kingdomprayer.org
or by fax at (770) 682-4301

For more information:
email info@kingdomprayer.org

Thank you for your prayerful consideration.